The ABCs of My Neuroses

Tales from an Anxious Life

JUSTINE CADWELL

Published by:
LIBRARY TALES PUBLISHING
www.LibraryTalesPublishing.com
www.Facebook.com/LibraryTalesPublishing

For general information on our other products and services, please contact our Customer Care Department at 1-800-754-5016, or fax 917-463-0892.

978-1-956769-35-7
978-1-956769-36-4

Contents

Prologue

Neurosis is the inability to tolerate ambiguity
- Sigmund Freud

An alphabetical structure is necessary

Because I crave organization and

Control,

Deriving comfort from

Everything having a discernable shape. What

Follows are tales about how

Genetics, life experience, and culture

Have

Influenced my neurotic tendencies.

Just so you

Know, diagnostic

Labels appear in this book but

My actions may

Not always

Operate according to every

Psychological definition discussed, as the lines between

Quirky behavior and mental disorders may blur.

Readers,

Some names have been changed in

These pages to protect privacy. Thank you for

Understanding. I am

Very excited (and slightly terrified) to put these

Words out into the world, but I hope my

eXperiences entertain you and expand your comprehension of mental illness.

Yes, it bothers me I didn't start that last word with "X." But I'm not a total

Zombie—you shall see.

Next time, won't you sing with me?

is for Avoidant

My worst nightmare is tantric sex: an ancient, sacred practice that involves *staring* into your lover's eyes during sensual acts. Just typing that sentence made me want to vomit. You know that old saying: the eyes are the window to the soul—or was it the Seventh Circle of Hell? I forget.

A sex therapist once commented how it's interesting I can talk flippantly about trying anal beads, but the mere mention of eye contact during sex immobilizes me.

Listen, you're *the doctor here.*

Suffice to say, I am painfully shy and insecure. Suffice to say, the last time I gazed into a lover's eyes without effort was after a deranged reunion during an abusive relationship. Suffice to say—I need more therapy.

During most daily interactions, I must force myself to make eye contact. The vulnerability of being *seen* unsettles me, threatens my confidence. As if I'm staring directly into a mirror in front of others, impairing my ability to hide from myself.

A typical grocery store encounter:

"Would you like your receipt, ma'am?" a cashier inquires. *Look at the human, Justine. You can do this!*

"No thanks," I reply, my shoulders tightening as I raise my eyes just long enough to meet theirs. *WTF is wrong with me?!*

Whatever this oddity is, I'm convinced it's at least partially genetic. My daughter has been saying "No see me!" since she learned the words. She also yelled "Nooooo!!!" as a crowd of family and friends tried to sing to her on her third birthday. We only like attention on our own terms.

§

My avoidant tendencies sprouted young. In the second or third grade, my class learned math using colorful blocks. My teacher wrote problems on the board, and we built visual answers, stacking the blocks to mimic addition and pulling them apart to simulate subtraction. One day, she noticed me goofing off.

"Justine, would you like to bring your answer up to the board?"

I froze and focused intently on the blocks laid out on my desk: yellow, red, blue, and green. I grabbed a structure built for a previous question and pretended the blocks would not come apart, as if someone superglued them together. To further sell it, I grunted struggle sounds. My teacher waited for a short while and sighed.

"Perhaps next time we'll pay attention instead of talking."

Then, she called on someone else, leaving me to my shame and patented approach to problem-solving: ignore it and it will (eventually) go away!

As a teenager, after a flirtatious night, I lied beside a boy in a dark room. Wandering hands slid across my body, but my limbs grew paralyzed.

What am I supposed to do? What if I do it wrong?!

Why isn't there a mandatory manual offered to every virgin, a how-to for alleviating sexual ineptitude?! I shifted my face toward the nearest wall and pretended to fall asleep. Better to just lie here, limp as a rag doll.

§

During my sophomore year of college, I started seeing a counselor for the first time. Depression brought me in, but I had experienced anxiety since childhood and suspected obsessive-compulsive disorder (OCD).[1] My completed intake paperwork left no stone unturned. The idea of putting all my mental woes into a professional's hands comforted me. *Here is everything that's wrong with me. Now fix it, please.*

My appointed university counselor was a soft-spoken middle-aged man who sported a George Costanza hairstyle and round Freud-style glasses. He explained my behaviors seemed more consistent with obsessive-compulsive personality disorder (OCPD) rather than OCD. "George" encouraged me to take a personality disorder test so we could (paraphrasing) get to the bottom of my endless neuroses.

---

1. OCD is an anxiety disorder characterized by obsessions and/or compulsions. More on OCD in chapter "I."

Symptoms of Obsessive-Compulsive Personality Disorder:

- Perfectionism to the point that it impairs the ability to finish tasks
- Stiff, formal, or rigid mannerisms
- Being extremely frugal with money
- An overwhelming need to be punctual
- Extreme attention to detail
- Excessive devotion to work at the expense of family or social relationships
- Hoarding worn or useless items
- An inability to share or delegate work because of a fear it won't be done right
- A fixation with lists
- A rigid adherence to rules and regulations
- An overwhelming need for order
- A sense of righteousness about the way things should be done
- A rigid adherence to moral and ethical codes

1. Perfectionism?
2. Extreme attention to detail?
3. An overwhelming need for order?
4. A fixation with lists?!

Well—okay, yes, that does sound like me.

I filled out the questionnaire, expecting George to deliver the news OCPD represented my biggest obstacle. Diagnosis meant definitive. Definitive > ambiguity. Instead, George expressed a new concern. My answers indicated I avoid uncomfortable situations.

Duh! Doesn't everyone?

Symptoms of Avoidant Personality Disorder:

- Avoids occupational activities that involve significant interpersonal contact because of fears of criticism, disapproval, or rejection

- Unwilling to get involved with people unless certain of being liked

- Shows restraint within intimate relationships because of the fear of being shamed, ridiculed, or rejected

- Preoccupied with being criticized or rejected in social situations

- Inhibited in new interpersonal situations because of feelings of inadequacy

- Views self as socially inept, personally unappealing, or inferior to others

- Unusually reluctant to take personal risks or engage in new activities because they may prove embarrassing

Feelings of inadequacy? Fears of criticism? Restraint within intimate relationships?!

Well—okay, yes, that sounds like me too.

George worried my actions (or lack thereof) might have some far-reaching implications in my life. Searching for a second opinion, I called my cousin Becca, a clinical psychologist. She had treated people with avoidant personality disorder. Over the receiver of my flip phone, she assured me a diagnosis was unlikely. In her personal and professional opinion, my behavior was not severe enough. People can exhibit the behaviors of a personality disorder without harboring enough dysfunction for a proper diagnosis.

My black-and-white rationality decided to dismiss the results of the test. No diagnosis, no problem? Of course, these patterns were troubling regardless. The smart course of action would have been to follow up with my counselor.

Nah.

§

Several years ago, I took an overnight trip to my old college town of St. Cloud, Minnesota, with my friend Gracie. I was still underage when I transferred to a different school, so this was my first chance to fully partake in the St. Cloud nightlife. Hoping to save money, we booked a hotel room with one queen-size bed.

Gracie invited her friend Eli to bar hop with us. We went to all the well-known spots, including The Press Bar and The Red Carpet Nightclub. Eli's buddy, Chris, joined us at The White Horse. Our bartender resembled comedian Marc Maron. A middle-aged man with a shaggy dirty-blond mane, groomed facial hair, and hipster glasses, he seemed to harbor Maron's moodiness as well. "Marc" practically proposed to me after I ordered a shot of Beefeater gin with water for a chaser, but his interest turned to disgust when I changed my liquor preference to vodka. I struggled to make small talk with Chris, shifting uncomfortably in our booth while Gracie batted her eyelashes at Eli.

Later that night, I cowered on my side of the bed while listening to Gracie and Eli get it on *in the same bed*. A normal person would stand their ground in this scenario. A normal person would get up and demand they knock it off right this instant!

"You're so wet," Eli panted.

Ugh! I played possum and tried like hell to fall asleep, ignoring the moans and musky scents to the best of my ability. The marathon sex session ended as the sun peeked through the blinds. *Finally!* I began to drift off. But then, one of the lovers emitted another obnoxious sound.

<ZZZZZzzzzz ZZZZZZzzzzz>

My eyes whipped open. Gripping my pillow, I stormed into the bathroom and attempted to utilize the bathtub as a bed. When that failed, I crammed myself into the backseat of my car. I grumbled and flung my body around, desperate for a comfortable position.

One whole hour of shut-eye under my belt, I sulked behind Gracie as we walked Eli home. I didn't confront my friend until later that afternoon. Even then, I refused to offer more than a vague annoyance: "*You* should drive us home, because *I* didn't really get any sleep last night."

§

I have a history of eschewing certain numbers: eating 12 almonds instead of 13 (the unlucky number), 7 M&M's instead of 6 (the devil's digit). While pregnant, I ascribed gestation weeks to the volume dial numbers on my CD player. Thirty-two created less anxiety than 24. I feared going too low might jinx my pregnancy and inspire premature labor.[2] To this day, I instinctively avoid the number 22. My high school boyfriend cheated on me on September 22nd. A few years later, my stomach sank as he pulled into parking spot 22 near First Ave in Minneapolis. We had tickets to see a show that night, but he got kicked out for being too drunk, and was robbed on his way back to the car. Coincidence? I think not.

§

---

2. These are classic examples of obsessive-compulsive behaviors.

Art imitates life. I procrastinated writing this piece because it would include humiliating confessions. Now the world will know how fragile I am. My flaws have been exposed. If Igor offered my Abby Normal brain to Dr. Frankenstein,[3] would the monster just lie there, too anxious in its foreign body to move a reanimated muscle? What a boring movie I would make!

Thank God this segment is over. Now I can finally get back to ignoring the reality of my avoidance problem.

---

3. It's pronounced Fronk-en-steen

is for Beauty

(RITUALS AND REVELATIONS)

Loving yourself is a full-time job with shitty benefits. I'm calling in sick.

                - *Samantha Irby,* Wow, No Thank You

I don't remember being self-conscious about my appearance before the age of 9. Prior to that, getting dressed represented a required step to climb aboard the school bus, my body simply the vehicle that carried me there. Circa the fourth grade, I started caring about the way my outfits looked while studying myself in the mirror every morning.

In middle school, I wore makeup for fun and the pursuit of looking older. However, by 13 my inhibitions escalated, and I decided with much certainty that I was ugly. Possibly the ugliest person who ever lived.

Reading fashion magazines and going through puberty had done their job. I concluded my looks were unacceptable: my thick, wavy blond hair was too fluffy, my pale Scandinavian face was too plain, and the gap between my front teeth (despite the popularity of Jewel and Madonna) was *not* sexy. I wanted the locks of Jennifer Aniston, the features of Natalie Portman, and the confidence of anyone else.

In our Midwest home, my older sister Louisa offered top-dollar spa treatments: $1.00 for a manicure, $2.00 for a pedicure. She rationalized the inflated price of the pedicure fair since she'd have to touch my icky feet. For $3.00, I purchased a fitness plan and lifestyle package, which included Louisa's best tips and tricks. She introduced me to *YM* magazine with covers featuring blond beauties like Alicia Silverstone and Gwen Stefani. Between Louisa and *YM*'s glossy pages, I garnered the wisdom to substitute hair conditioner for shaving cream, apply toothpaste to zap zits overnight, and stuff scented dryer sheets in my underwear drawer for maximum freshness. Part of my exercise plan included a daily date with our mom's *Abs of Steel* VHS. After several weeks, we both sported enough core definition to impress dedicated gym bunnies.

Around the same time, *Clueless*, one of my favorite movies, displayed gorgeous teenagers with large closets and a knack for makeovers. I knew what had to be done. I made a list of what to buy to become beautiful. I leafed through *Seventeen* and *Jane* periodicals, scrutinizing every page. Featured products were added to the list. Each advertised brand made the cut. If a specific lipstick was mentioned in a DIY makeup tutorial, my pencil moved. Every time I purchased an item off my list, I gained an ounce of control, crept one inch closer to total desirability.

I smoothed foundation over my pimple-free porcelain skin, bought warming clay masks, shady infomercial products (Nads hair removal system anyone?), and expensive eye creams. I used my allowance to buy Herbal Essences, as fruity-scented hair was sure to get all the boys. Maybe my mom found satisfaction in her cheap 2-in-1 Suave cleanser, but *I* was above that.

During English class, my friends giggled as I applied layer upon layer of several lip balms and glosses. Soon enough, perfection would be mine. An advertiser's dream, I fell for every pitch. "Clean and Clear and Under Control," "Easy Breezy Beautiful CoverGirl." Step right up, step right up! All you need is an endless supply of money and zero self-esteem.

I developed my own extensive rituals: washing and moisturizing my face every night, plucking my eyebrows on a regular basis, and weekly pedicures involving vibrant shades of polish. Chilled cucumber slices and frozen spoons were used to banish those pesky undereye bags, an apparent teenage epidemic. Once a week, I shaved my legs with a brand-new razor. Then I slathered my skin with Warm Vanilla Sugar lotion from Bath and Body Works. The Olsen twins would never be caught dead with stubble on their legs during one of their exotic adventures. So, by God, neither would I. Every Sunday, I spent 2-3 hours primping and priming, starting each week of school as a new and improved ~~girl~~ woman.

A crush of mine told me he would like me more if my teeth were straight.[4] Around the same time, my dad broke the news that I would not be getting braces. I cried while interrogating my dad, creating a scene in the downtown shop we were in. I guess my parents didn't mind ruining my life just because braces weren't a "medical necessity" for me, as they had been for my sister.

Fortunately, during my early high school years, I began growing out of my self-conscious angst. In school, we started a unit focused on branding and marketing tactics: how advertisers use fear, sex, and bandwagon appeals to trick consumers. A meaningless, superficial image was being sold

---

4. Really, Tom? *Really?!*

to me—on purpose! I still wanted to be pretty, but hell if that meant giving in to these swindlers!

I continued to follow some of my beauty routines but shifted focus. Instead of acquiring more lengthening mascaras and a posh wardrobe for my path to enlightenment, I became intrigued by the promises of healthy and authentic living. I purchased a book called *Mind, Body, and Soul: The Body-shop Book of Wellbeing*. It featured illuminating content about toxin elimination, reflexology, and meditation. Apparently, circulation and hydration were key, prompting me to ask for (and receive) a Brita water filter for Christmas.

In health class, I gave a report about the dangers of tanning beds, insisting vanity was not worth the risk of skin cancer. My mixed media collage for art class featured a photo of the '90s sex symbol Brittany Spears. She was scantily clad, had a large yellow boa constrictor draped over her shoulders, and of course flaunted a deep tan. Surrounding this image, I pasted phrases about the faulty feminine ideal, with heavy words like "truth" scattered around the periphery.

By the end of high school, punk culture enchanted me, and the pages of fashion magazines completely lost their shine. I shunned the intricacies of traditional beauty standards, deciding they were for fools. I wore hemp necklaces and washed my hair intermittently, my makeup routine simplified: black mascara, coral blue eyeliner, and plain lip balm (no gloss).

The rebellious recordings of bands such as Rage Against the Machine and Fugazi started blasting out of my room. Their lyrics were full of wisdom and offered new profound mantras by which to live.

"You are not what you own."

I determined a meaningful life expanded well beyond the expectations of society, and my body was just a vessel to carry me through it.

I wasn't treading water in the kiddie pool anymore. I was *so* deep.

§

Nobody warned me about this.

Immediately after turning 34, my hormones went haywire. Suddenly, cystic acne erupted on my chin and cheeks, the type that hurt like a motherfucker, cannot be popped, and leave scars in their wake. I noticed darker, coarser body hair and…*is that a mustache?! When did my chin hair get this long?!* Oh, and did I mention the chronic yeast infections?

Happy Birthday to me, Happy Birthday to meeee!

Apparently, the dirty thirties often arrive with some undesirable baggage. When estrogen drops, there is less competition for androgens, so testosterone traits are more likely to be expressed. Riddle me this: what use is a libido boost when I feel like a pizza-faced yeti with an itchy vagina?

A ghost from my past encouraged me to regain control over the situation. I am not a smoker or a wino, and I do not drink coffee on a regular basis, but that doesn't stop me from buying teeth whitening pens. Lumify eye drops, which brighten eyes better than traditional eye drops do, cost about $20 for 0.25 ounce—but—*I need them.* My skin care routine has evolved into a part-time job: face wash, eye cream, vitamin C serum in the morning (for fine lines), moisturizer, tinted mineral sunscreen for my face, retinol serum before bed (for acne and post-acne scarring), body scrubs, and cocoa butter lotion for my legs and abdominal stretch marks.

Thankfully, my dermatologist helped me get my acne under control by stabbing my face with expensive needles. After a *year* of monthly yeast infections, boric acid suppositories prevented me from detaching my vagina and throwing it into a river. But this hair ain't goin' anywhere unless I remove it myself. If I were a better feminist, I would stop shaving altogether, but I'm too brainwashed by American culture to pull it off.

Last year I bought an epilator, which rips hair out by the root, to use on my legs. It hurt. A LOT. But no worries, it was all worth it. I ended up damaging my hair follicles! Also, I flirted with a new manifestation of my OCD, known as trichotillomania, in which I spent endless hours hunched over my legs, tweezing out individual hairs in a compulsive manner to deal with uncomfortable feelings. Now I have the pleasure of enduring endless ingrown hairs and unsightly red blemishes that invite alarmed, "What happened to your legs?!" reactions.

Once upon a time, I had tiddies. Now, I have mammary glands. I am bothered by the fact that my boobs are not perfectly symmetrical, that my left one has the audacity to take up more space than the right—or maybe I'm mad at my right boob for not being as large as my left boob? My nipples used to be smaller, a lighter shade of pink. I regret not taking several high-quality pictures of my tits before letting my daughter chew on them for 18 months straight.

While repeatedly hitting the refresh button during an online search for secondhand clothes, I ponder Einstein's famous quote about insanity. But if I keep looking, maybe I'll discover a magical dress that can transform me into my best self. How will I find it if I give up the search?

I am not one to body shame others, but I've always struggled to forgive *myself* for being a human being. I want every unsightly hair removed, every undesirable scent deodorized, and every potentially sexy feature amplified to 11. Give me perfection or give me death!

I think this is the part where I insert some inspirational words about loving your body the way it is, but all I can offer is this. Underneath my rekindled desire to present myself in an attractive manner, I also have the wisdom to know I am bullshitting myself. This body, no matter how I decorate it, remains an unruly earthly vessel. Recently, I've stopped caring about walking around the house naked with the windows open, mostly out of laziness but also because, it's just a body, dude.

And well, that's something.

is for Cemetery

For kids especially, making something scary 'fun' offers just enough distance to engage with it, make it feel a little more in their control*, and make them feel like they have gained a sense of some mastery over something unknown.*

- Margee Kerr, sociologist

As a child, I oscillated between sheer terror at the idea of my own mortality and a morbid fascination with death. My best friend Kelsey and I attended Riverside Elementary in Moorhead, Minnesota. Our favorite recess activities revolved around death. We designated certain areas of the school playground as heaven, hell, and purgatory.[5] We assigned our hell section on the side where more kids tended to throw up, demonstrating a solid understanding of evil.

Kelsey and I roamed around looking for random piles of leaves, gathered by the unruly prairie winds. Then we took turns using our hands to brush the leaves aside until reaching the asphalt.

---

5. *One* of us was Catholic—okay, it was me.

"Ah yes. This is the grave of my dead brother who tragically died in a plane crash."

On the school bus, we regurgitated scenes from horror movies we couldn't unsee: Pennywise ("It") the clown causing blood to rain out of faucets and shower heads, Freddy Krueger coming to murder you in your dreams. Kelsey confessed she was afraid to put on her sock, worried Freddy would pull her inside it. It was dark in there! She also told me about a book she read, featuring the "true" story of a haunted playhouse in which a plastic oven mysteriously caused water to boil and scald an unsuspecting child.

At my house, we plopped on pillows in front of a large blaring box fan and pretended to fly through clouds on magic carpets. Occasionally, I turned the fan off, simulating a pit stop in heaven. Then I'd flip the switch, resuming the blast so we could continue our celestial journey.

We both loved watching and rehashing episodes of the Nickelodeon classic *Are You Afraid of the Dark?* We were intrigued by the little girl trapped in the mirror, the swampy skeleton living at the bottom of a boarded-up pool, and the cigar-smoking clown who harassed a boy for stealing his nose.

In an episode featuring '90s celeb twins Tia and Tamara, a chameleon takes the form of a girl after biting her. During a pivotal scene at the end of the episode, the girl's best friend must correctly choose who to kill: her friend or the chameleon pretending to be her. Kelsey and I decided we better come up with a secret name in case we happened to find ourselves in a similar situation someday (likely instigated by me). We chose "Amy," but that's classified information I'm entrusting you to keep quiet in the event of a lizard invasion.

§

In my living room, my friends and I turned out the lights and told ghost stories beside a "campfire": a large red flashlight, clicked on and posed toward the ceiling. I seem to remember even grabbing some marshmallows to roast over the imagined roaring flames. With a little more imagination, we might have taped some yellow construction paper to the bulb cover and sprinkled some wooden blocks as kindling, but I'm not sure we ever got that far.

Sprawled out on the cushions from the pull-out couch, we listened to my older sister Louisa read snippets out of her *Goosebumps* books. *One Day at Horrorland* described an amusement park whose "fake" monsters seemed a little too real. We passed around *Scary Stories to Tell in the Dark* and even generated a few improv tales of our own.

§

On Halloween, my dad helped Louisa and me create custom tombstones out of scrap wood and cardboard. We spray-painted them gray and scrawled out epitaphs using permanent black markers. My mom added a few drops of green food dye to my Campbell's chicken noodle soup for an extra ghastly dinner.

At the age of seven, I dressed up as a vampire: white face paint, black vinyl cape, and cheap plastic fangs sullied by fake blood. My costume was based on the most convenient examples of the era: Dracula and Nosferatu. These scary pale creatures slept in dark coffins to avoid the light of day. In the early '90s, vampires were still a scary force to be reckoned with, not romantic figures who sparkled in the sun.

The same year I went as a vampire, we assembled a haunted house in our basement for a party I hosted. My dad worked at NDSU Extension and brought home a large gray photography backdrop which served as part of the enclosure. Our soundtrack consisted of a spooky sounds CD compilation, full of grumbling, feasting demons and their startled, unsuspecting victims.

I laid a "trap" at the bottom of the stairs, a plastic mat turned upside down to expose the spiky underside. My sign painted in pink glow-in-the-dark paint was plastered a few feet above, telling lurkers "I'd turn back if I were you."[6] A fake leg dangled from the drop tile ceiling. I provided the unfortunate disclaimer that we were beneath our front yard cemetery, and body parts were known to make an appearance.

I fastened a cat mask to a mirror and cautioned my guests from staring into it if they didn't want to transform into a black cat themselves!

My pet monster hid behind a wooden puppet show contraption. We set a meaty dog bone in front of it for my friends to marvel at. Meanwhile, my dad hid behind the scenes, forcing a shaky clawed arm through the curtains. Nearby, a glass of "blood" sat beside a doll, strangled to death by a vicious snake (which bore an uncanny resemblance to a ribbed vacuum hose).

"Don't get too close!" I warned.

§

At our neighbor Amanda's house, Louisa and I toyed with a Ouija board. A circulated rumor implied a person should never use one alone, because you might become possessed! Using the board with a small posse meant greater safety, so this was the only way I was willing to give in to my curiosities.

Did we want to know when we would die? Several brave souls who explored eternal wisdom with their fingertips posed this popular inquiry. I wanted nothing to do with it. Who would want to be privy to such information?! Instead, I chose questions that seemed harmless, unlikely to upset the

---

6. *The Wizard of Oz* reference

spirits or myself.

"What is the name of the man I will marry?"

The marker moved toward H. Then, E.

"Are you moving it?! I'm not!" I said.

A...

"I'm not doing anything. I swear!" Louisa insisted.

T...

"I'm not pushing it either," Amanda chimed in.

H...

The spirits destined I would marry a man named Heath. After further probing, I learned we would have a proper brood as well: two girls and one boy.

To end the suspense, I must confess my husband's name is Derek and we only have one daughter. In high school, I tried to make sense of the premonition. Did we contact the ghost of a poet who preferred metaphors to literal interpretations? The dictionary definition of "heath" indicated a barren wasteland. Sometimes this definition seemed to fit my high school boyfriend. But alas (and thank God), I never used that as an excuse to marry him.

Here are other possible explanations I've come up with:

1. At least one of us lied about moving that Ouija piece. (I refuse to believe it!)

2. The spirits were lying or misinformed.

3. Maybe our ghost struggled with spelling and meant to suggest I would marry "health" since I grew up to be a dietitian?

These days, I like to assume I was meant to spend a beautiful life with Heath Ledger, but his untimely death put a kink in our pre-sealed fate.

§

At my Aunt Lori's house, I played the yard game Ghost in the Graveyard with Louisa, my cousins, and some neighborhood friends. A small patch of forest bordered the large backyard. This area was off-limits—which was fine by me! I remember the blend of fear and excitement as I hid behind a bush waiting to be discovered by a mortal. Pretending to be a ghost gave me a certain sense of invincibility. Becoming the monster you fear can take away some of its power. If you can't beat 'em, join 'em, eh?

§

I once had the brilliant idea to stage my own death, convinced I could trick my parents. Cutting a domed headstone out of paper, I marked it with all the important details: "Here lies Justine..." This was placed at the top of my "body" fashioned out of blankets. You think I left it at that? I wasn't an amateur! I put my sneakers at the bottom, clearly indicating it was me who had passed. On a cassette tape, I recorded my voice singing Chopin's Funeral March:

"Duh dut da da...dut dah dah dah dah duh duuuu..."

Then I cleverly hid behind the couch, playing my recording whenever someone descended the family room steps.

Shockingly, no one bought it.

is for Depression

"...my quirks had gone beyond eccentricity, past the warm waters of weird to those cold, deep patches of sea where people lose their lives."

— *Emma Forrest,* Your Voice in my Head

PHQ9 Depression Questionnaire: Over the last 2 weeks, how often have you been bothered by any of the following problems?

Feeling down, depressed, or hopeless

Once upon a time, depression held me captive, and I developed Stockholm syndrome.

After I graduated from high school, I moved to a new city in Minnesota to attend St. Cloud State University. My boyfriend Romeo moved in with me and became my primary social outlet. This was unfortunate, because we were both introverts with a capital "I." Even though I attended a "party school," we never went to any parties. We hardly spoke to anyone outside of work and classes. Instead, we spent a lot of time only with each other. A liability, as we both suffered from depression.

Gloom saturated the air of our microcosm. I became so used to the dark I didn't know how to respond to a glimmer of light. A trick? An illusion? This dreadful demeanor broke into my being. Contrary to an unwelcome guest, depression registered as an integral part of me. *There is no silver lining. Everything is terrible. You're not good enough.* My captor plastered these bumper stickers to my brain as I attempted to focus on survival.

Thoughts that you would be better off dead or hurting yourself in some way

Life was bleak, stagnant. Romeo had recently been robbed at gunpoint while delivering a Domino's pizza, and my response surprised and scared me. No concern. No sadness. *Nothing.* For me, the worst shade of depression is neither sadness nor irritability. It's apathy. Feeling numb is terrifying. It necessitates teetering between extremes to verify one's status as a living, breathing being.

One night I locked myself in our apartment bathroom. I began a staring contest with my razor, perched innocently on the edge of the dull yellow tub. My mind floated near the island of my body, detached. I wished to translate my mental anguish into physical evidence. I chose a discrete area, on my upper inner thigh, and pressed the blade into my skin. A hint of blood, a stinging sensation: proof of my existence. Through pain and precision, my disconnected self reunited, if only for a moment. I went back for seconds.

A few days later, Romeo took notice of my battle scars and confronted me. *My razor attacked me,* I had practiced over and over in my head, convinced I could halt the discussion with such a declaration.

"My razor attacked me," I said, nonchalant.

I didn't want to lie, but I didn't want to tell the truth either. I hoped he would chalk it up to careless shaving. Romeo seemed suspicious, but let it be.

Eventually, I confided in him. Part of me (enamored by my captor) wanted the cutting to remain a secret, a private torture just for me. But the other part of me (my actual self) knew it was a cry for help.

"I cut myself," I said, letting out a few tears.

"I will always be better than you, because you did that," Romeo retorted with disgust.

His words cut deeper than the razor. I needed a friend. I needed support. But after his calloused reply, he agreed I should probably speak to a counselor soon.

Counselor: "I've noticed you laugh a lot when you talk about these really horrible things that have happened. That must be how you cope with them."

Damn, he's on to me.

Counselor: "Maybe you'd like to consider taking some antidepressants for a little while?"

Yeah, maybe.

By this point, depression was old hat to me, but my self-harm signified worsening symptoms. I didn't like the idea of needing a pill to feel normal, but after my counselor brought it up, pharmaceuticals became a reasonable solution.

A toxic environment left me stranded. I needed to escape my living situation, turned hostile by harsh words and hard alcohol. I talked about my relationship struggles with Romeo. The counselor pointed out how I kept letting things go to see if they would get better:

Counselor: "It's as if you have your hand on a hot stove and you're just waiting to take your hand off."

Taking an SSRI anti-depressant medication[7] helped me cope until I could move out of the apartment I shared with Romeo. This drug did not serve as a panacea, but it gave me hope. It allowed me to recognize the beast of depression as a separate entity from myself, one who did not deserve my admiration. The romanticism of melancholy melted away. I weaned myself off my anti-depressant medication, confident it was no longer necessary.

§

Trouble concentrating on things, such as reading the newspaper or watching television

Shortly after graduating college, I started working at a library. This seemed like the perfect fit for an avid reader and writer. The first year floated by like a dream. I loved finding new books to take home while rummaging through the returns. Using the scanner to check items in and out reminded me of playing library in my home den as a kid. Shelving served as a fun, satisfying challenge (have I mentioned I'm a nerd?).

But after a while, the shine wore off. The tasks I enjoyed turned into monotonous chores, and I feared my brain might be turning into mush. Instead of concentrating on my work, negative thoughts looped in my head: *Life is meaningless. What's it all for? Why bother?* These pessimistic blurbs were always available on tap, trickling out during times of boredom. Quitting became imperative to preserve my mental health. I searched the Internet for any job I might qualify for, entertained the idea of a pay cut. The most important thing? Learning something (anything!) new. I needed a different environment, with fresh puzzles for my mind to solve.

---

7. Generic Lexapro, I believe

§

Trouble falling or staying asleep, or sleeping too much

As a young adult, my doctor diagnosed me with asthma. My albuterol inhaler (a stimulant) combined with fear-induced symptoms made quality sleep illusive. My lack of sleep inspired more anxiety, which spiraled into an endless nightmare of monitoring my breathing as I struggled to differentiate between hyperventilation and a true asthma attack. I needed a professional to explain the difference to me.

I sought a second opinion from my mom's doctor. I broke down crying during my appointment, succumbing to my fried nerves. The appointment took an unexpected turn when the doctor presented a depression questionnaire. I filled it out but insisted I was not depressed, just ill and desperate for answers.

"You circled suicidal thoughts."

This is a great example of problematic perfectionism. I had *one* suicidal thought *one* time, and it went like this: *At least if I were dead, I wouldn't have to feel this scared all the time.* Done. End scene. I did not envision my demise. I did not plan out how I would do it. But because I needed to be 100% honest with 0% ability to explain myself, I left without a solution to my original dilemma and with pills for a different problem.

Instead of prescribing the anti-depressant which worked for me in the past, I was given a new and improved brand which claimed to produce fewer sexual side effects. Within a few days of starting this medication, my mood took a serious nosedive. I shifted from a mild melancholy to a terrified, hopeless state. I didn't have suicidal thoughts, but I sensed their menacing shadows within the walls of my psyche. The insert said to stop taking this medication if my depression got worse. So I did.

When I told my mom's doctor, he shook his head and insisted I didn't give the medication a fair chance. That's when I decided to give up on doctors, opting for the anxious headspace where I still didn't really actually want to die.

§

They say money can't buy happiness, but that's not exactly true. When money buys you food, shelter, warmth, and health insurance, it buys you a less stressful lifestyle, and that can lead to vicarious happiness. My husband Derek and I have come a long way from hoarding macaroni and cheese packets to stretch into separate meals (him) and keeping the thermostat under 60 degrees to save money (me). Still, our improved circumstances do not guarantee a depression-free existence.

No one is immune.

§

Poor appetite or overeating

Seasonal Affective Disorder (SAD – how appropriate), a depression related to seasonal changes, is difficult to dodge when you live in the tundra. It took me years to finally commit to a therapeutic light box meant to treat it. Every winter I would create an excuse not to get one. I can't afford it! Okay, now I can, but how do you pick one? There are *so* many to choose from. I was pummeled by decision fatigue while reading reviews. And when would I use it? Staying seated in the same place for a half-hour seemed impossible with a toddler running around.

For several years, my SAD coping system revolved around food binges. Usually ice cream. Pints and pints of ice cream. While this approach is less detrimental than drug abuse, I can't recommend it. I gained weight and lost confidence. My guts rebelled. The instantaneous relief always melted into shame by the final bite.

§

Moving or speaking so slowly that other people could have noticed? Or the opposite – being so fidgety or *restless* that you have been moving around a lot more than usual

This is my process. I boggle ideas around my head while obsessively cleaning every nook and cranny. Who needs their senior yearbook? Toss it in the garbage. Why did I ever buy this shirt? Throw it in the donation box. Eventually my surroundings sparkle, and I'm left with the exhausting task of further distraction. I panic when I run out of mazes for my mind to navigate. The pressures of the here and now are too great.

Derek told me he would quit smoking by the time he was thirty. He continued to smoke after his thirtieth birthday came and went, so I decided to bump up the pressure. Derek prefers my hair long, so I presented an ultimatum: quit smoking by x date or I will shave my head. It was a win-win scenario for me. Either Derek would drop his unhealthy habit, or I would get to scratch this itch that seemed to come out of nowhere.

Since I had been old enough to make decisions about my hair, I generally kept it long enough to cram into a comfortable ponytail. My boring library job left me fiending for a drastic change, and the idea of making a radical *Fuck ideal beauty standards* statement intrigued me.

"Just make sure you aren't doing this because you're depressed and desperate for something to change," my friend Kelsey said.

"Oh no," I replied, matter of fact. "That's exactly what this is."

Derek didn't quit smoking by my predetermined date. Giddy with excitement, I invited my friend Nicole (my go-to hair gal) to help with the transformation. When my long blond locks were replaced with a light stubble, I felt lighter, badass even. I enjoy bold experimentation, and I didn't (really) regret it. But once the final strands of hair fell to the ground, the best part was over. The high wouldn't last. My feelings of emptiness simply had a hairstyle to match.

§

Feeling tired or having little energy

"Would you like to see a magic trick?" Depression asks.

"From you? Uh—thanks I'm good." I reply.

But Depression has never respected my wishes and proceeds to suck all the energy out of each crevice of my body until I'm hollow.

"Voila!" Depression announces with satisfaction. "Now, get to work! Remember you have to do this for the next 40 50? years until you can afford to retire. *Hahahahaha*. Good luck with that in this economy! But don't worry, thanks to climate change, you and everyone you love will probably be dead by then anyway. *Wink wink.*

Little interest or pleasure in doing things.

I spy half-empty glasses everywhere I turn. "What's wrong?" the world wonders, asks with concern. Nothing is *wrong*. Things just rarely feel right and when they do, the moment is fleeting. On a few occasions I've experienced a blissful stillness in which all felt right in the world. A genuine Nirvana on Earth: here one second, gone the next. Where did it go? What made it happen in the first place? Can I harness that energy? Recreate the perfect symphony of neurotransmitters and circumstance? I don't suppose I can, but what else can you expect of a pessimist?

What is the secret to mining enough satisfaction from the simple things— a freshly mowed lawn, a recipe gone right, the rare social gathering with friends— to render the doldrums of life bearable? I crave validation, endorphin-fueled encounters, love, drugs, music, and grand gestures of martyrdom. Maybe I should have died during Woodstock.

Kelsey texts me a Reductress article: "Jealous? This leaf just died."

I laugh, thankful the universe brought us together. "I am jealous," I reply.

"Me too."

§

I have seen a few counselors for brief stints over the years and some were more helpful than others. Recently, my therapist asked me why I insisted on suffering when I could take a medication to help me.

"I'm used to suffering."

I have chronic pain, so this is true. But I was also scared. I worried I wouldn't be able to orgasm anymore (a valid SSRI fear and something I already struggle with), that music would stop giving me goosebumps (per a Reddit post I once read), that I would turn into a zombie, uninterested in taking care of my child (per a friend's Zoloft experience). I worried about gaining weight and having more digestive issues than I already experience (thanks IBS!). I wondered what the point was. My default genetics are always going to point toward anxiety and depression and the idea of being on anti-depressants for the rest of my life doesn't sound sustainable or safe to me.

Despite limited research on the potential hazards of long-term use, doctors are overzealous in the prescription of anti-depressants. Depression, like all mental illnesses, exists on a continuum. Depending on the cause and severity of a person's depression, anti-depressants can be lifesavers or colorful band-aids.

For example, one symptom of undiagnosed Celiac's disease is depression. Celiac's disease is an autoimmune disorder in which the body attacks its own intestinal lining in response to gluten ingestion. A person with undiagnosed Celiac's disease is likely to have intestinal damage which reduces the absorption of certain nutrients, nutrients which are necessary for creating neurotransmitters. In other words, a doctor may offer anti-depressant pills to a patient who would experience more effective relief from dietary changes and nutritional supplementation.

§

In his book *Lost Connections: Uncovering the Real Causes of Depression—and the Unexpected Solutions*, award-winning journalist Johann Hari, identifies nine causes of depression:

1. Disconnection from meaningful work (see: library job mentioned above).

2. Disconnection from other people (see: living alone with depressed alcoholic boyfriend in a strange city).

3. Disconnection from meaningful values (see: materialism encouraged by a capitalist society).

4. Disconnection from childhood trauma (see: health insurance plans that prioritize physical healthcare over mental healthcare).

5. Disconnection from status and respect (see: structural sexism, racism, ableism, and ageism).

6. Disconnection from the natural world (see: cutting down forests to build strip malls, calendars hung in stale, windowless cubicles featuring shiny green palm trees illuminated by fluorescent lights (not sunshine), and rainbow-colored plastic debris collecting

along shorelines).

7. Disconnection from a hopeful or secure future (see: people working three jobs for the pleasure of living paycheck to paycheck).

8 and 9. Genes and brain changes: (see: G is for Genetics and Celiac's disease example listed above; recognize that genes require triggering circumstances, and no one is doomed to a life of depression simply because they harbor the genetics that make them more susceptible).

To me, depression has always felt like an appropriate response to the modern world. And it seems I'm not wrong. The author of *Lost Connections* interviewed Laurence Kirmayer, the head of the Department of Social Psychiatry at McGill University. Mr. Kirmayer stated that the current psychiatry model prefers to focus on the biological side of depression (see: chemical imbalance theory) because it is 'much more politically challenging' to acknowledge that the roots of depression stem from the seeds planted beneath our feet: how our current societies are structured.

§

On the other hand, both my sisters who share similar mental afflictions swore by their antidepressants, a recent episode of uncontrollable crying seized me during a drunken state, and Rome wasn't built in a day. My therapist framed the option in a favorable, non-threatening light: use it, for a brief period, as an adjunct to therapy. Anti-depressants may make therapy easier and more effective. Research indicates that being on an antidepressant for as little as a year may have the ability to create lasting, beneficial changes to my neurotic neural network.

In the words of the wise prophets Gene and Dean Ween, "Give me that Z-O-L-O-F-T."

I started taking Sertraline[8] about a year ago and—it's been amazing. Catastrophizing is no longer my default response to life, I can socialize with strangers without wanting to die (usually), "simple" tasks like going grocery shopping don't feel as laborious, and I'm *gasp* pretty happy most of the time? Being medicated helps me engage in the behaviors that bring me happiness and encourage well-being, such as finding the motivation to exercise, write, play music, and volunteer. This world is still fucked but instead of feeling overwhelmed with dread, more brain space is dedicated to focusing on the things I can change versus obsessing over the things I cannot.

Why *did* I insist on suffering?

§

Feeling bad about yourself – or that you are a failure and have let yourself or your family down

My friend J's sister suffers from depression. J has never dealt with it personally and confessed her frustrations with her sister's odd and selfish behavior. I explained how depression paralyzes a person, turning them into an altered version of themselves. I suggested her sister seek professional help. J seemed hopeful but hesitant, unsure if her sister could be convinced to do so. Unfortunately, I've witnessed this resistance in others (including myself). Without hope or motivation, it can be easy for a person with depression to talk themselves out of treatment options. *What's the point? Do I deserve to feel happy? Is it even possible?*

After Robin Williams committed suicide, I read accusatory online comments: *How could he be so selfish? What about his family, his children, the fans who looked up to him?* But Robin likely believed his family, and the whole world for that matter, was better off without him. This is one of depres-

---

8. Generic Zoloft

sion's favorite lies.

I've been intimate enough with depression to understand how difficult it can be to stand your ground against it. I've teetered close enough to depersonalization to understand how alluring suicide can become.

§

In Sylvia Plath's *The Bell Jar*, the main character Esther retreats to the bath as her depression seeps in. Eventually her depression leads to severe insomnia, suicide ideation, hospitalization and electroshock therapy.

While wallowing in a hot bath during a vulnerable night, I wonder: *Is this how my final descent into madness will begin?* The feelings of hopelessness so visceral at times, they swim beside me. I worry about my daughter, potentially caught in the undertow.

§

I'm lucky my anti-depressant medication works for me. The reality is these types of medications are only effective for some people in certain situations during specific times. It's not uncommon for people to try several anti-depressant medications before finding the one that works for them, and even these drugs may lose effectiveness over time. Side effects may cause more distress than the presenting depression symptoms, prompting a person to stop taking their prescription. Occasionally, drastic measures like ketamine infusions and electroshock therapy are needed to keep depression at bay. And sometimes, people don't have access to the therapy they need or sufficient treatments aren't identified in time. Too often, loved ones are lost to this terrible (systemic) disease.

§

Depression scoffs at me from the Sertraline sidelines,

"I see you are in a good place now. Well, don't get too cocky.
I know where you live."

No one is immune to depression—

and acknowledging that is part of the cure.

𝓔
is for Ethics

During college, I worked at Subway and wrote an exposé research paper about the restaurant chain. Titled "The Big and Hearty Contradiction," my paper called out the hypocrisy of their promotional double meat subs. I drove a tack through my paper, attaching it to the bulletin board which held our posted schedule. The first paragraph illustrates the tone of the piece:

Hearty, as defined by Webster's Classic Reference Library Dictionary, is an adjective which is meant to describe something "nourishing." One might expect this term to be used to describe healthful foods, such as homemade stew. Whatever one may picture when the word hearty is mentioned, it is unlikely anyone would imagine a heaping sub of meat and cheese which packs on more calories than a McDonald's Big Mac. Surprisingly, Subway, a company that loves to boast about how "healthy" it is in comparison to other types of fast food, offers more than just one of these heart-attack-on-a-bun options.

My convictions were too strong to be stifled by the possibility of getting fired.

I had recently read the book *Natural Cures "They" Don't Want You to Know About.* I couldn't believe all the things "they" were keeping from the American people! I found myself captivated by the detail-oriented path to optimum wellness, but I did what most people do when they adopt a new dogma: I picked the parts I liked and ditched the rest.

The *Natural Cures* author, Kevin Trudeau,[9] encouraged colonic irrigation on a regular basis. I relished the idea of perfect intestinal cleanliness. But having a giant tube inserted up my rectum with the intention of flushing water up into it? No thanks. On the other hand, I agreed the FDA sounded more like an enemy than an ally. I also pawned my microwave to avoid eating tainted food, dangerously transformed by its radioactive rays. (Insert eye roll.) In addition, the main message of Trudeau's book struck me: "It's all about the money." The revelation that Big Pharma and Big Food relied on keeping people sick to grow their profits blew my mind.

My obsession with *the truth* took on a new persona with this fresh information. I scoured the library for books and watched several documentaries to educate myself further. The book *Excitotoxins: The Taste That Kills* (not alarmist at all…) informed me how aspartame destroys brain cells. So much for Diet Coke being a healthier option. *In Defense of Food* introduced me to profound dietary scripture: "Eat food. Not too much. Mostly plants." *Food Politics* exposed the corruption within the food industry and the American Dietetic Association.

The Future of Food documentary included a horrifying "revolving door" scene, which exposed numerous government officials with industry ties. This movie also introduced me to a monster named Monsanto, a corporation guilty of suing

---

9. This guy is currently in jail for fraud, btw

small farmers over seed patent infringement. The film *Food Inc.* made me even more passionate about avoiding factory-farmed meat.

All this food research was inconvenient as I was studying to become a registered dietitian at the time. I was 20 years old in 2007 and attending North Dakota State University in Fargo when I started traveling down this alternative route. The more self-study I did, the more I questioned the facts my professors expected me to accept. Once I learned the food guide pyramid had more to do with the work of food lobbyists than the promotion of health, anger fueled my determination to spread the word.

At Subway, I loved ranting to my coworkers about the hypocritical message we were selling: "Eat fresh." Ha! I started collecting the ingredient lists of our products, intending to write a thesis about it. These facts disgusted me:

> 1. The Italian white bread contained traces of mineral oil (a laxative).

> 2. Our pickled veggies glowed neon bright because of food dyes.

> 3. The first ingredient in our honey mustard was "high fructose corn syrup" (not honey, not mustard...).

> 4. The roasted chicken "breasts" boasted faux grill lines painted on their exterior.

In a successful attempt to woo me, my soon-to-be boyfriend Derek gave me *Food Additives: A Shopper's Guide to What's Safe & What's Not* as a gift. This book allowed me to connect each questionable ingredient with its potentially harmful effects. For example, I noted "caramel color" was a suspected human carcinogen. Therefore, in my mind, eating the roast beef at Subway basically equated to asking for cancer.[10]

I started making homemade whole wheat bread, feeling self-righteous about its healthfulness. I brought this bread and organic cheese slices to work to assemble veggie sandwiches with as little processed product as possible. On one occasion, my boss helped a customer while I made myself a sandwich:

"Oooh what kind of bread is that?" the customer inquired.

"Oh, that's just a special bread..." my boss said, dismissive.

"That's the special?!" the customer exclaimed.

"No, no..." my boss continued, trying to explain one of his employees brought in their own bread by choice. (Fantastic marketing, eh?)

I became fixated on achieving a perfect whole-foods diet. I even wanted to cut out all refined sugar. Honey, maple syrup, and molasses were okay, however. *At least there are nutrients in those* I reassured myself. Living a life free from the shackles of processed foods didn't seem unreasonable, even if that meant being a loon about it. I tried to cut out as much factory-farmed meat as possible. Broke as a college kid joke, I still insisted on making organic, free-range meat and wild-caught fish a priority in my budget.

The vegan diet gave me a complex. Was it the one true lifestyle or a false prophet? The proponents claimed vegan diets were the best for animal rights, personal well-being, and the environment. But it bothered me most vegans probably weren't 100% true to their diet. I discovered some food additives were derived from animal products. Even pure white

---

10. In 2014, a food blogger petitioned the company to stop using azodicarbonamide as a dough conditioner. This same "ingredient" is used in the production of yoga mats. Subway has made several ingredient changes since this time, seemingly prompted by public pressure.

sugar could be processed using bone char! Possessed by black-and-white thinking, it was easy for me to dismiss the overall goal of the diet by pointing out tiny possible flaws. If a person was only 99.9% vegan, why bother? An advantageous conclusion: I could keep eating butter while feeling superior in my deep knowledge on the subject.

Beyond my overwhelming mix of actual and pseudo-scientific health research, I also strived to stop supporting bad companies. *The Better World Shopping Guide* became my Bible for how to spend my money. Walmart got an F for promoting anti-union policies and setting poor environmental regulation standards. Mars Candy Company shamefully used child slave labor in their candy production. Nestle employed deplorable marketing strategies. The corporation's reps traveled to developing nations, trying to convince new mothers that formula represented a healthier option than breastmilk, even in villages lacking a clean water supply.

I vowed to shun the attire produced in sweatshops and buy second-hand clothing as much as possible. By 2009, I conducted thorough research before buying most products. No more animal-tested shampoos! Out with the laundry detergents containing phosphates! It was an exhausting rabbit hole to have fallen into, considering how many small companies are acquired by large corporations.

I couldn't buy Silk soymilk, because Silk belonged to an evil company called Dean Foods, which owns some of the largest factory dairy farms in the country. Tom's of Maine seemed like a good choice for fluoride-free toothpaste until I discovered Colgate-Palmolive, a company that still tests on animals, bought them out. I would drive to three different grocery stores in pursuit of specific moral products. I hunted for Humane Raised and Certified chicken breasts and Fair-Trade Certified bananas, coffee, and chocolate. It was not lost on me the amount of gas I used to acquire these environmentally friendly products. Making the *most* ethical choice seemed like a battle that couldn't be won!

After several years of fighting the good fight, I allowed myself to chill out. In fact, there are two cartons of Silk soymilk in my fridge right now. Martyrdom appears to be my default mode, but I could no longer carry all the stress of our planet's future on my shoulders.

I still make a valiant effort to be a responsible consumer. I recycle, eat a plant-based diet, and vote for politicians who neither deny nor ignore the climate change crisis. Trying to make the world a better place is much preferred to idly sitting by while plastic clutters our oceans. But doing the right thing also means having compassion, and these days I make sure to leave some for myself.

is for First Love

Could any two souls, any alcoholic and codependent, have collided and produced this exact tragedy? Probably. Like the monkeys locked in a room who eventually write Shakespeare. The grief over the end of the relationship is nothing compared with the mourning I must do for the thing I long believed to be love.

— *Nina Rinata Aron,* Good Morning, Destroyer of Men's Souls

The first time I fell in love, I hit the pavement on my way down. I offered my entire being to someone with no concept or care of how dangerous that could be. Convinced I was meant to be with this person, I created excuses to stay despite getting slapped by red flags around every corner. I decided he was a good person (deep down), so I accepted that his words often spoke much louder than his actions. Because at times, he spoke such beautiful words.

§

The star of my affections was Romeo, an emotionally disturbed teenager (just like me!), but his baggage was heavier than mine. I was 16 when we met in my friend Skyler's garage. Skyler lived in a shitty apartment in south Fargo. Due to the embarrassing amount of clutter Skyler's aunt acquired over the years, Skyler kept us quarantined in the garage. Here, we were always up to mischief. We'd close the door and pass a bowl while listening to Nine Inch Nails. Then light some incense and open the door to let in the sun.

Romeo arrived with his best friend, dread-headed Kent. I offered him a VHS case to crush whatever white pills lay before us. Romeo possessed long-lashed hazel eyes with dilated pupils and shaggy dirty blond hair. The combination of black thick-framed glasses and his prominent nose made me want to have sex with his face.

My friend Jake challenged me to infiltrate Romeo's world and free him from his girlfriend. I knew a couple things about Romeo at this point. He did DXM ("robotripped")[11] almost every day, and he had a "crazy" girlfriend named Liz.

I loved the idea of saving Romeo and making him mine. I am an avoidant person by nature, but with electronic communication, there's no need to be coy. The first instant message I remember sending Romeo: *You should break up with your girlfriend.*

Romeo broke up with Liz after weeks of encouragement. Most of our initial correspondence took place through IM chats, and my attraction grew as I learned more about him through these conversations. A sexy non-conformist with big ideas and passionate emotions? Just my type!

We made plans to go to the mall. I picked him up in my green dimpled Dodge Intrepid. Inside we searched for nail polish. He purchased a shiny green color for himself called

11. Drinking Robitussen cough syrup to get high

"Envy." (Note: Poetic foreshadowing.)

Back at home, I listened to the CDs he burned for me. Big mistake. Quickest way to fall in love with a boy who's no good. During the B.R. (Before Romeo) era, I primarily listened to soundtracks, popular radio songs, and greatest hits compilations. I felt refined for owning the Beatles 1 album. But Romeo introduced me to music that was eclectic and seductive, opening my eyes to a whole new world.

I loved the defiance in Zac de la Rocha's voice, the morbid lyrical stylings of At the Drive-In to the beat of unique instrumentation, and Denali, a band whose magic lied in Maura Davis's melancholic tones. A boy who can appreciate sad girl music? Is there anything better? Music spoke to me in a way no other art form could match. I sensed love in the cards after discovering Romeo and I both spent our evenings listening to Radiohead's *OK Computer* on repeat before our paths had even crossed.

January 2004

Reyna's house served as a "freak" refuge: a sanctuary for cutters, homosexuals, and neurotics. I picked up Romeo, and we headed over to Reyna's birthday bash. He had just eaten a handful of nutmeg.

"What's it like?" I inquired, amazed at the concept of a cooking spice containing hallucinogenic potential.

"It's weird. You have to eat a lot of it though."

I didn't intend to ever try it.

Upon arriving at Reyna's, we scattered in opposite directions. An ex of his named Kylie spent a chunk of the evening trying to weasel her way back into his favor. Meanwhile, I hung out with my other friends. Romeo left his long wool coat (no doubt a Savers find), radiating Old Spice on a couch in Reyna's room. I found solace lying on it, trying to absorb his essence. I could have lived in that coat.

Toward the end of the night, Romeo started crying, trashed after several drinks. Kylie brought him into a spare bedroom for some coddling. After I couldn't take the suspense any longer, I let myself into the room. Kylie glowered at me and left. I stared at Romeo, with his bloodshot, watery eyes and looked down at my knock-off converse tennis shoes. *I belong here, right?*

"Nobody cares" Romeo pleaded.

I didn't understand the babbling surrounding the context of the statement, but it didn't matter.

"I care," I promised. I hugged him close and drove him home.

Two Days Later

Romeo played his guitar with a feverish diligence and impressive skill. To my adolescent mind, he embodied the epitome of the holy trinity: sex, drugs, and rock-and-roll. He represented a modern Buddy Holly my raging hormones could not resist.

We flirted on Romeo's bed in an unorthodox manner, playing tug-o-war with a plastic shelf leg. I leaned in to kiss him, and serotonin singed my spine. A degree of warmth I didn't know existed filled my entire body. Our tongues danced to Aphex Twin while I floated in place. Holy shit was this boy going to be trouble.

On my way home, my fuzzy head failed to compete with the icy roads, and I crashed into a cement barrier. Shaken and shivering, I left my car stranded and headed toward Skyler's apartment, a few blocks down. He helped me fix the flat tire and sent me on my way. If I believed in divine intervention, I might have assumed someone was trying to tell me something. *You are headed down a dangerous path.* However, I didn't heed any warnings. I headed home, toes and fingers freezing but my spirit on fire.

§

February 2004

I sipped on a green apple Jones soda at Kelsey's house.

"I lit the candle," I confessed.

Kelsey's face lit up, "The love candle?!"

"Mhm."

"Yay!"

Years before, I had purchased a candle on a band trip to Winnepeg. It contained three layers of color: red, yellow, and white and smelled fresh and fruity like a budding romance. "The first time I fall in love, I will light this candle," I told my friends, harboring a desperate need for symbolic gestures.

Romeo and I had only been dating for one month, but it was official: I was fucking doomed.

After school, one blustery day, I showed up at Romeo's house. He wouldn't answer when I called from my car. What now? Was *she* inside?

Romeo had warned me about Liz. She often invited herself over, punched in the garage code (still off-limits to me), and snatched the spare key to let herself into his condo. Never mind the fact Romeo had ended their relationship months before.

Shivering on the doorstep, I mustered the courage to ring the doorbell. I waited several minutes. Finally, Romeo yanked the door open.

"Guess who's here?!" Romeo said, a wild fury in his eyes. He stepped aside to reveal the infamous "crazy" Liz standing at the top of the stairs. I studied her small frame, pulled-back dark hair, and checkered Vans sneakers. She scowled at Romeo as she stomped down the steps to leave. Liz and I had never met before, and I'm sure Liz would have preferred we never meet again. The feeling was mutual. But neither of us would get our wish.

March 2004

Romeo and I walked to Cash Wise, a local grocery chain. I bought a box of Wheat Thins and a bag of Peachios. I saved the receipt because I noticed the date was March 19th, our two-month anniversary. Romeo smoked the Marlboro cigarettes he routinely stole from his dad's stash as we meandered through alleys with billboards and talked about nothing.

Nothing = everything, in his company.

Later that evening, we sat on Romeo's dining room floor. My eyes followed the looming chair shadows climbing up the walls.

"You have to be careful," Romeo said. "Liz is fucked up."

"If anything happened to you…" Romeo's voice trailed off into a land of disbelief.

§

(Excerpt of a typed letter from Romeo)

Justine,

You are beautiful to me in every way a person could be. Everytime i think about you i cant help but smile, thats a really nice feeling lemme tell ya…its really hard to be with out you…even if it is for only a few hours or whatever. sorry if that sounds creepy…its not ment to. it just hurts, ya know? i always feel that when we are together that i cant get

*close to you...even if we are laying right next
to each other i feel like there's still miles between us physically. i feel like youre the other
half of my brain sometimes. perty damn cool
if i do say so myself. i love you justine, you
make me the happiest guy around. it makes
my day when i see you smile :-P. goodnight.*

I love you

-Romeo

§

April 2004

In an email, Romeo told me he loved me, I was beautiful—
and we had to break up.

Liz had a reputation for being a compulsive liar. Around the
end of their relationship, Liz claimed to be pregnant. Romeo
stored this information under the mental compartment "typical Liz," another pathetic attempt to keep him within her
clutches.

As time marched on and Romeo and I became more entan-
gled, Liz's vines sprouted actual roots. She *was* pregnant. I
was too in love to leave Romeo over this one (baby) bump
in the road, but he felt the need to be there for Liz. It was the
"right thing to do."

This breakup crushed me into dust. I became a zombie, wad-
ing through the motions of life out of habit. Jake noticed a
new hollowness in my eyes, previously brimming with life:

"Justine you've got to let go. You can't go on like this!"

Romeo had become my entire world in just three months.
I might as well be dead. Why bother? When the entity you

have built your existence around ceases to exist, there is no longer a desire to live.

One week later we were back in each other's arms.

May 10th, 2004: The Day Liz Died

While preparing to leave for my 4pm Subway shift, my phone rang. *Romeo!*

"Hey!" I answered.

"Liz is dead."

"What?!"

"Liz is dead," Romeo replied, monotone. "I've gotten all these messages from her grandma and dad saying I put her under too much stress. She went into premature labor and died during delivery."

I was speechless. This young teenaged girl, alive one minute and gone the next. Part of me viewed the situation as tragic, but a louder, immature voice promised *We're free!* What kind of monster wishes death upon someone? I guess I didn't *wish* it, but I certainly welcomed it. Romeo would never be all mine while under her spell.

"I'm so sorry, Romeo." For him, I was. He lost his first love and potential mother of his first child. I glanced at the clock. "But I have to leave for work now. I'm going to be late."

"Okay. Call me later."

An hour or two into my shift, Kelsey stopped by with her new boyfriend, Cory. I grabbed a broom and headed over to their table. Word had already gotten around.

"This is messed up," Kelsey said. "I can't believe she's really dead!"

"I know," I replied, forcing the broom under the table next

to theirs.

"How is Romeo holding up?" Cory asked.

"Not well. I think he might feel partially responsible. At least, that's what her family is trying to make him feel."

My coworkers must have overheard our morbid conversation. They let me leave early, presumably to deal with whatever teenage nonsense I needed to attend to.

At Romeo's condo, the messages came in waves, but in my memory, they never stopped. One phone call would end and the next would begin. Sometimes, someone would just call and hang up: Liz's classic move (see "typical Liz" brain file). One message came from Romeo's friend, Ike, offering his condolences.

Later, Ike stopped by in person. As the voicemails trailed on in the background, Romeo's frustration reached new heights.

"She's not dead you know," Romeo said.

"She's dead dude," Ike replied.

Romeo shook his head.

"What are you talking about?" I said, annoyed with his denial.

"Her 'aunt' and 'uncle' stopped by to rub in her death too," Romeo continued. "I recognized both those Fucks. The girl is one of her friends, and the guy I remember from South." [12]

Romeo began to describe them. Contorted characters, reminiscent of *James and the Giant Peach*, appeared in my mind. The boy stretched unnaturally tall and thin, with a long poignant nose and a disgusting black hairy birthmark on his neck. The girl possessed a round figure and boring facial features. A fuzzy pink sun hat cast shade upon her forced

---

12. Romeo's high school before he dropped out

melancholy expression.

The theme of these reports: Romeo ought to be sorry for what he put Liz through. He bore sole responsibility for her death.

Would Liz pull a stunt like this? Mutual friends had verified Liz's manipulative nature, claimed she often managed to get people to bend to her will. But *who would do such a thing?* She must be dead. Right?

Late that night, an unidentified South Dakota number showed up on Romeo's caller ID. "It's Liz," Romeo said with eerie confidence. He let the call go to voicemail. *Click.*

May 11th, 2004: The Day Liz Rose From the Dead

The next day, I skipped school to be with Romeo. *He needed me* I reasoned. Around ten in the morning, Romeo and I cuddled on his bed.

Knock! Knock! Knock!

Romeo bolted out of the room to see who waited at his front door. Hesitant, he stepped out onto the balcony. "It's Liz," he grimaced. *She is fucking crazy!*[13]

"You should hide in the closet," Romeo said.

REALLY fucking crazy! I quarantined myself in the living room closet, shutting the solid wood door behind me. Romeo descended the stairs of his condo to confront Liz at the front door. Muffled shouting boomed from the stairway, the words gaining clarity as they moved closer to my hiding space.

"You pretended to *die* Liz!"

"I was in the Cities. People did this behind my back!"

Sunlight streamed in from a nearby window, shining a spot-

---

13. I'm no longer a fan of this reductionist term, but as a teenager, "crazy" was still a part of my regular vocabulary.

light on the carpet beneath my feet. The warmth of my surroundings clashed with the chaos of the moment. *Is this a normal thing to be doing?*

During my childhood, I once sought shelter in my grandma's basement during a thunderstorm. My cousins and I crowded together inside a musty closet. While tornado sirens roared outside, we shined a flashlight onto a glow-in-the-dark haunted house book. I preferred natural disasters and illuminated ghouls over scary ex-girlfriends.

More shouting in the stairwell. A slammed front door.

Silence.

After a few more minutes of quiet, I cracked the door open and peered around the living room: empty. I walked to Romeo's room with an air of confidence, soon crushed by the silhouette of a dark-haired girl sitting on his bed. *Fuck! She's still here!* I rushed back to the closet, only to be released by Romeo a moment later.

"Dude, it's safe now," he said with a giggle.

"Oh," I answered. "Who is here then?"

"That's my friend Kaitlin. We made plans to hang out today, before all this bullshit started."

Detroit Lakes – June 2004

After a steamy make-out session in my dad's basement, Romeo and I snuck off to a Perkins diner in the wee hours of the morning, all hopped up on lust and love. While digging into my pancakes, Romeo said the words I had been waiting to hear.

"You don't have to worry about Liz stealing me away." He continued, "You don't have to worry about *anyone* stealing me away."

Romeo won me over early in the relationship with his "Parents don't understand real love" balcony speech.[14] We were both the product of broken homes (or divorce in middle-class terms) and believed we knew more about REAL love than they did. Romeo described how meaningless sex was, well, meaningless.

What conclusions could a young girl come to? Between his passion towards passion and denigrating himself by relating to the song "Creep," I needed to jump his bones as soon as possible. The idea my skin could make anyone cry was too flattering to ignore.

Are you ready for me to try stuff? Romeo inquired over instant messenger, a few months into our courtship. Hell yeah I was.

Getting Romeo to have sex with me became a quest. When he and Liz were an item, they promised each other they would never have sex with anyone else and he took this vow seriously. Instead, Romeo and I fooled around, engaging in multiple failed attempts to go *all the way* while naked and vulnerable in front of each other.

§

Relationship-isms

"Nothing will ever be okay ever" we often barked at each other with a sarcastic tone and a smirk. It played on our understanding of the world. We were two miserable people with the ability to reach unthinkable levels of happiness when the other was around.

I loved holding Romeo as close as possible and saying "mine" as if to suggest I could possess another human being. He reciprocated with the same level of eagerness and desperation. Who knew people could survive a significant

---

14. No, really. We were on a balcony.

portion of their lives with only half their being intact? What prompted our hearts to beat before these moments?

§

June 2004: A River Runs Through It

River Emma Einrich was born. Romeo spent the afternoon visiting Liz and River in the hospital. That evening, a storm brewed a few miles away as we walked to a nearby park.[15] We held hands as fat raindrops fell onto our backs. When we arrived, we sat in the swings, forcing the wind beneath us, practically daring the distant lightning to strike us. Drunk on the birth of his child, Romeo spoke of his instinct that River would be a "daddy's girl."

A lovely fantasy, but we would only see River on a handful of occasions.[16]

September 22, 2004

Liz convinced Romeo to sleep with her. Considering he harbored pent-up emotions, a daily drug habit, and teenage boy testosterone levels, it was no chemical anomaly. But it didn't jive with my Romeo schema. My brain couldn't comprehend how a person I could trust with my life couldn't remain faithful under the most trying of circumstances (manipulative ex meets raging hormones). Romeo tried to break up with me again, rationalizing he ruined everything between us—but I wouldn't allow it. I fought too hard for too long to gain his attention, and I wasn't about to let her win. *We can work it out.*

---

15. A place we often went to have deep conversations and pretend we were adults

16. Eventually, River (and the other baby...keep reading) was taken away from Liz by social services and put up for adoption. Romeo and I were relieved. He wasn't ready to be a father, and he knew Liz didn't have the capacity to be a responsible parent either...as evidenced by her past behavior and the report the social worker sent us indicating unsuitable living conditions.

I delved into a deep, numbing depression. I bottled up all my hurt, my rage. Writing became my only release. I wouldn't tell anyone about Romeo's descent from perfection. His reputation would not be tarnished if I had anything to do with it! I kept associating my ability to breathe with his presence in my life, even as things turned irreparably sour.

January 2005[17]

§

When I returned from a family trip, Romeo gave me a hand-written letter.

An abridged excerpt:

> *Justine,*
> *You're amazing. Before you I thought it was normal to be kept on a leash (smell the glove)[18] and be told how I felt about this that and the other thing. You give me a sense of*

---

17. Some emo art I created on a trip with my family. Romeo and me at a show in the basement of our local VFW. The lighter shading in Romeo's profile was meant to represent Liz's residual influence. How deep was I?

18. *This is Spinal Tap* reference

*freedom and that I can go and do what I
please without losing you. I feel that the more
I am myself the more you love me. I know I'm
stupid at times and yet you still accept me.*

*You make me want to be a better person so I
can give to you what you give to me, or maybe I can give to you more than what you give
me. My mom always tells me that you're a
blessing from God, and the more life goes on
the more I believe her. You're beautiful Justine.*

*I love you,
-Romeo*

§

"It" finally happened two days before our one-year dating
anniversary. Losing my virginity was uncomfortable and
unimpressive. I blame Hollywood for setting my standards
artificially high. But sex grew more pleasurable over time.
Oxytocin poured into my brain, creating more perilous delusions about our inability to be anything but made for each
other.

February 2005

I thrived on Romeo's jealousy. My recurrent mentions of a
new coworker made him paranoid. Jim was a cool cat. Our
friendship was sparked by the Modest Mouse pin Jim spotted on my purse. We had a lot in common, and he was a
music fanatic like Romeo and me, so I often brought him up
during conversation. My attraction to Jim seemed insignif-
icant. Jim was married, and I had finally captured Romeo's
full attention.

Romeo and I had our own world. Which lovers don't? Romeo felt threatened, as if someone meant to intrude upon his

territory. One day, he told me about a dream he had. During the dream, Jim tried to steal me away, and Romeo murdered him. His masterful storytelling and intense eyes captured the anger, the sadness, the loss. *Nobody* was taking his girl away! Only a fool in love could be flattered by such an account, and I was. Heavy and unforgiving, his envy made me feel special. Whatever power Liz held over him, on some level, he truly was *all mine.*

But soon, Romeo's jealousy turned accusatory and smothering. It became less romantic and more like another obstacle our courtship might not survive. We watched Pink Floyd's *The Wall* together. He interpreted the main character's relationship with his wife as a parallel to our own relationship. I struggled to convince him of the difference.[19]

§

A hand-written letter from Romeo (an abridged excerpt)

Justine,

I'm sorry for the way I've been lately. I can't say that enough. I believe you when you say you've been faithful to me, and I'm VERY deeply sorry for ever doubting you. I don't know what's gotten into me, but please know that I am making a conscious decision to throw all those thoughts away.

Justine, I want to be yours only, and you to be mine for as long as we live, even beyond. I don't know where I'd be if you hadn't come into my life,

---

19. His wife cheats on him while he's on tour. Sure…just like us.

I don't want you to feel that even tho I've said all that I have that you have to stay with me. You are your own person with your own needs, want, goals, all that, so just follow what you think is right, and if it sucks for me than I'll deal with it.

I just want you to be free to do whatever you wish, and if that means being with me than that's awesome, and if not than that's awesome too. I will support you in whatever you want to do to the best of my ability. I love you my angel.

-Romeo

§

The cheating episode of September fucked with my head, made me question our relationship. I grew weary of settling Romeo's paranoia about my imaginary transgressions against him. Still, these doubts failed to motivate me to walk away from the love of my life. Until March...

March 2005

A normal day at Reyna's: people cluttered her filthy porch puffing away at their clove cigarettes, bitching about the status quo. Kelsey and I sat on the grass in front of the porch discussing radical appearance possibilities. Admiring the natural kink in my knotted wavy hair, Kelsey assured me, "You should totally get dreads." Jake agreed.

Hours later, after everyone had moved inside, I noticed an incoming call from Romeo. I excused myself onto the deserted porch to answer.

"Hey you!" I exclaimed.

"Hey," Romeo replied, monotone.

"What's up?" *Something is wrong.*

"Liz is saying she's pregnant again."

"Bullshit! If she's been pregnant since September, she would have brought this up *way* earlier."

"Yeah…"

"What, you don't think so? Come on, you know how she is!"

"I can't do this anymore."

"Do what?!" *Please don't break up with me!*

"I had sex with Liz while you were in Florida.[20] Obviously you're going to leave me now." *Click.*

After Romeo hung up on me, I held the silent phone to my ear. My heart stood still. My brain stopped working. My gut went sour. I slapped on a poker face for my friends and casually excused myself to leave. Once inside my car, I mourned my illusions of happiness. I screamed from the top of my lungs, tears flowing down my face the entire drive over to his house.

When I entered his bedroom, all hell broke loose. I sobbed on his floor. He wailed on his bed and begged for my forgiveness.

"Obviously, we have to break up Romeo. How can I ever trust you again?!"

He threw Griddles,[21] a stuffed bear I had given him, a symbol of all that had been good, at my limp body. He knew how

---

20. My family trip back in January

21. The previous May, I bought Romeo a teddy bear after his wisdom teeth were removed. The tag said his name was "Griddles." We thought this was hilarious, comparing a stuffed furry friend to a pancake appliance, so the name stuck.

to hit me where it would hurt.

"Take this with you then! I'm moving to Colorado, and you'll never see me again!"

My eyes ached, my steadfast resolve faltering. *What if I lose him forever? He's my soulmate!*

"Or maybe I'll just drink this whole bottle of lacquer thinner tonight and then neither of us have to worry about it."

"Romeo don't!" I begged.

Through weepy bloodshot eyes, he dared me: "WHAT DO YOU CARE?! YOU WANNA LEAVE!"

All rational thoughts of ending the relationship came to a screeching halt. I swept up the puddle I had melted into and stared at Romeo with sad eyes.

"I care," I promised.

§

The day we both went looking for each other

I insisted upon a break as my compromise, enjoying the freedom of having the upper hand. I needed time to process all I had just learned. I felt paralyzed, a prisoner in my own body. I was not blind to the injustice of it all, but when all was said and done, I always came to the same dangerous conclusion: this is love.

I lasted four days.

After school on the fourth day, I drove to Romeo's condo. His dad answered the door and told me Romeo was at "the park." I knew which one. I went there to find him. Turns out, he had been looking for me too.

§

Staring at the bus schedule plastered on Romeo's bedroom ceiling, I pondered the sad accuracy of the Portishead lyrics as they filled the room:

Cause nobody loves me, it's true...not like you do

§

A hand-written letter from Romeo (an abridged excerpt):

Justine,

You make my life worth living. Everyday you get more and more beautiful. I think that love is putting you before me, and I know I haven't been doing a good job of that, and I'm VERY sorry for that. But with time and you as a good role model, I'll show you I love you more than any one in this world can. The whole world could melt in front of my eyes and wouldn't care as long as you were holding my hand. I love you, Justine, I can't say that enough. Just like kissing you, it never gets old. I love you, Justine.

Love,
Romeo

§

Grown-Ups Now

June 2005

"Dude, we signed a lease today!" Romeo exclaimed with such bright-eyed anticipation it made me smile.

It was official! We would share an apartment together in St.

Cloud, MN where I would attend college in the fall. From this point forward, we would be more than high school sweethearts. We were grown-ups now, ready to leave our past behind us. Off to the great unknown land of adult living. We would be grocery shopping and paying rent. We could sleep in the same bed every night, and nobody could say a damn thing about it or do anything to stop it.

Money was tight initially. I didn't start my work study job right away, so we cleaned apartments together for extra cash. One month, Romeo mysteriously had money for a gram of coke but not for rent. On a dry-erase board displayed on the fridge, I kept a tally of all the rent he owed me, denying my passive aggressive approach when confronted.

Our evening routine involved watching the Game Show Network, particularly *Lingo*, while eating spaghetti or hamburger helper out of our cheap orange plastic dishware. On weekends, we turned Uno into a drinking game. We got drunk and remolded our hearts into magnets, despite whatever drama enveloped us, or perhaps because of it.

Misery Loves Company

I obsessed over the dates of Romeo's falls from grace: September 22nd, January 7th, September 22nd, January 7th, September 22nd, January 7th…

I handled our time together through a hefty amount of journaling and poetry writing. In a weird way, I relished the torture: a budding artist after all. I discovered falling in love was remarkably easy but staying in love was tougher than they made it look in the movies.

I tried to escape my morbid thoughts by submersing myself in my classes. It's not impressive that I received a 4.0 my first semester. It's the natural outcome of an obsessive person pouring all their energy into memorizing information. I closed the door to our "office" and stared at the pages until

I practically knew them by heart. Every so often, Romeo let himself into the room to lay across my books, vying for my attention with sad puppy dog eyes.

"Puuupppyy," I reprimanded him. "I'm busy with homework."

For the record, I was almost always "busy" with homework.

Romeo started drinking more…and more…and more. We grew apart. We were both depressed… alone… together.

August 2006

The exact moment I realized the gravity of the situation. Romeo's friend Kent came to St. Cloud for a visit. As the evening progressed, Romeo's eyes morphed in a fashion I had come to despise. The transformation was complete. The alcohol controlled him now. He went into the bedroom on a rampage and grabbed his pink guitar labeled with a "Pork" sticker, intent on smashing it into our TV. Kent and I pleaded with Romeo to relax, but Romeo had left. Instead, a monster stood in his shoes. He cornered me in the kitchen and shouted in my face. Romeo's utility knife gleamed in the distance, and Kent hid it as I made desperate eye contact with him.

Help me!

Kent tried to reason with Romeo, but you can't reason with a person in an irrational state. Romeo eventually backed down and headed out the door with the disclaimer he was going to the quarry to kill himself. After he stumbled out the door, I looked to Kent, shaking with horror.

"We need to call the police! He's going to kill himself!"

More interested in getting us the hell out of there, Kent insisted we leave. I told him I had nowhere to go. Somehow in this scenario, I allowed Romeo's safety to take precedence over my own. My biggest concern was not self-preservation.

It was maintaining my balance atop the pedestal he put me on. I was afraid of losing this status, of finding out I would always feel empty without it.

January 2007

I headed home to celebrate the new year with Kelsey and Cory. Romeo elected to stay behind. *Good!* I needed quality time with my friends, minus the steady pressure of my relationship. Outside of Romeo's grasp, a burden lifted.

On New Year's Eve, Romeo called, interjecting pessimistic blurbs into my previously carefree evening. He was fucked up on something, and I couldn't stand the idea of another disagreement. After a guilt-ridden goodbye, Romeo continued to call. Again…and again. I turned off my phone, needing to ignore the hell that had become my life and immerse myself in the positivity of the occasion.

The following morning, I had ten plus voicemails from Romeo. I gasped at the sheer volume of missed calls and started the taxing endeavor of listening to my messages.

"I've taken a bunch of pills...I think I'm dying," Romeo slurred.

"Mom!" I cried, rushing out of my high school bedroom.

My mom called Romeo's dad as I called Romeo's phone. Again…and again.

Ring….

Ring….

Ring…

No answer.

Oh my God, oh my God, oh my God!

Ring….

Ring....

Ring....

No answer. Straight to voicemail.

Ring...

Ring...

"Yeah?" answered Romeo, annoyed.

"Why didn't you answer your phone?! I thought you were dead!"

Romeo shrugged off my concern. He was angry we took the initiative to involve his dad.

"I thought you were dead!!"

§

Trapped. Romeo remained an unbearable force I could not manage, and yet I couldn't imagine an existence without him. Status quo melancholy allowed such insanity to become our normal. I morphed into a masochist. I didn't know what a healthy relationship looked like or whether I deserved one in the first place. A touchy volcano, Romeo spewed negativity at any random shift in momentum. I lived at the bottom, pondering escape but ultimately choosing to stay. This rock, after all, was my home.

May 2007: Escape

At the end of the semester, I planned to move back home, transferring from St. Cloud State to North Dakota State University for dietetics. The plan, as far as Romeo knew: he would stay behind to wait out the lease, and we'd reunite back in Fargo. My secret plan? I would take all my furniture, tell him it was over, and that'd be that!

But you know how that broken record goes by now, don't

you? We said a tense goodbye, my resolve shattering as I drove away. I called Romeo's phone after reaching the interstate. *Maybe just a break for now?*

§

After Romeo moved back to Fargo, we tried to make things work in a new environment. He lived with Kent, and I rented a house with Kelsey and Cory. But this extra space only showed me how much relief his absence brought. So, we broke up (a fourth time).

February 2008

Remember Jim? You know, that married guy from work Romeo was paranoid about? By this time, he and his wife had divorced. We spent a lot of time partying together with friends and ended up dating for a short time. Jim treated me well, and we had a lot of fun together. We smoked weed and listened to Tegan and Sara. We wrote each other love letters that included song lyrics rather than apologies. Unfortunately, my emotions were so deranged by this time, I didn't know how to handle it. I giggled awkwardly when he wanted to cuddle in a quiet room and cringed when he said my name during sex. *What is this strange phenomenon called romantic affection? I think I'm allergic to it.* I broke Jim's heart to continue abusing mine.

May 2008

I moved into a tiny efficiency apartment, one of four units in a house. My good friend Megan and her husband Markus lived below me on the main floor. They treated me like family, allowing me to borrow their spare car when mine broke down and feeding me delicious vegetarian meals on the regular. Is this what love is supposed to look like? Unconditional kindness? What a concept!

This was my first time living alone, and with my friends close but not *too* close, it was the perfect arrangement. I could party downstairs and then head up to my apartment to recharge. My newfound independence helped me trace the space where Romeo ended and I began.

Instead of allowing Romeo to rant about *everything* under the sun, I started to challenge him. He mocked my nutrition major, the fact I adopted a habit of listening to public radio, and eventually, my new friends. I don't remember what he said about Megan and Markus that set me off, but I remember thinking *Oh no you don't. Not them. They've been nothing but wonderful to me.* In addition, my college education and greater awareness of the world allowed the depths of his ignorance to grow more apparent. It seemed I was growing up and he was stuck in Neverland.

I sensed the end was near but needed to gain the resolve to end things (for good this time).

July 1st, 2008

The final night before smoking in the bars was banned in downtown Fargo, Megan and I went to a show, got drunk, and had a great time. The next morning, I decided to sweat off my hangover by biking to the Farmer's Market. I was in a fantastic mood on this beautiful, sunny day. Romeo and I touched base while I shopped. He was working, delivering pizzas that day. We agreed to meet up in between deliveries.

I locked my bike to a picnic table and climbed into Romeo's car with a smile on my face. Immediately, Romeo's reel of negativity scrawled toward the passenger seat. I kept my cool and positive attitude despite it, utilizing my newfound skills to tune out his bad vibes. Somewhere along the drive, we started arguing. I don't remember why we fought, but I remember the final moments, when I realized it was time.

"Do you think we can both live our lives the way we want to and still be happy together?" I asked.

Romeo paused, ceasing his barrage of complaints. I assume

he sensed the severity of the situation because he lied out of desperation.

"Yes."

"Well, I don't. I think we have to break up."

§

April 2010

Weaning was difficult but I finally succeeded in moving on with my life. I spent many afternoons haunting the symbolic cemetery of my relationship with Romeo. I went to "the park" to grieve, hoping to catch a glimpse of a ghost I missed. I didn't expect or wish to run into Romeo, but to reoccupy a space that had come to define me in such a profound way brought comfort. These grounds helped mitigate recurrent panic attacks as my endorphins attempted recalibration.

Maybe I was looking for clues. Clues that would help me make sense of it all. A bridge between the excitement of adolescence and the doldrums of adulthood. Or buried treasure. A relic of years past that would teleport me back to a time when my life had such esoteric meaning. At one point, it was palpable. I touched it, and it felt amazing in a way no other experience could impinge upon. Romeo was my witness... and he felt it too. Goddamn. Ignorance really was bliss. Never mind the battle scars.

Several months after we broke up, I reached out to Romeo to initiate hanging out and hopefully gain closure. It was hard at first. Codependent relationships can be addictive, and we both still harbored unresolved feelings toward each other. But the passage of time served as a balm for our wounds. Romeo embraced sobriety after a bout of alcohol-induced pancreatitis nearly took his life at the age of 21. New lovers shifted our focus away from each other and Romeo and I made amends, reconstructing a friendship out of the rubble of our past.

§

February 19, 2011 – An {Abridged} Letter to Romeo

I wish we could be a bigger part of each other's lives, because I consider you a lifelong friend. I want you to know I have a greater understanding of the things that happened to a larger capacity than ever before. I understand the power Liz held over you (your first love), because I've felt the same power you've possessed over me. I understand how you were unable to be responsive towards me during your heaviest bouts of depression. I've felt that demon come over my brain and know its hold. I understand the drive your addictions created, because I've been an adult long enough to understand the allure of a vice. I've been hurt by these things but don't really blame you and forgive what's happened. I'm proud of how far you've come in conquering these difficult obstacles. I believe our relationship to have made a connection between two like souls that may never be broken. I hope your life dreams are realized, and you won't be afraid to call on an old friend when times are tough. I love you in a purely platonic way. (Me and Julian…we got one of those plutonium kinds of love[22]…haha)

<3 J Crew Catalogue [23] (Fall Edition)

A written reply from Romeo (an abridged excerpt)

---

22. Trailer Park Boys reference

23. A nickname Romeo liked to call me by

Dear Justine

You know, or at least you should know, how much you mean to me and how much I care about you. You were my bestest friend and irreplacable. You always will have a spot in my heart. And I mean always. I've never felt that way about someone before and I don't know If I ever will.

I would love to have more of a friendship with you because that'd just be awesome. And that's an understatement. But it's entirely up to you and how it flows with your life and your relationship with Derek[24].

I'm sorry my letter isn't as in depth as yours, but I'm sleepy and feel stupid. If you want to talk about it sometime, I'm always here.

-Romeo

§

I found it hard to let go of my first love but harder to release the fantasies that shaped our union. In the end, I grieved less over losing my soulmate and more over the affirmation no such thing exists.

I often miss the rush of infatuation, but even the steamiest affairs are doomed to fizzle out over time. From 16 to 35-years-old, my conclusions surrounding love have evolved: It should not be one-sided or driven by ego. Sharing values is more important than sharing musical tastes (though, for me, some overlap is necessary). A broken heart is not always synonymous with a broken spirit. And most important: if you can't live with or without someone? Leave.

---

24. My boyfriend at the time (and eventual husband)

True love is more complex than the glittery version selling greeting cards. And while it may be a bit lackluster, it's more genuine at its core.

FIRST LOVE SOUNDTRACK
DISC 1: INFATUATION

1. *El Scorcho - Weezer*

2. *You File - Denali*

3. *Kiss Off – Violent Femmes*

4. *Flim – Aphex Twin*

5. *Away and Anywhere – John Frusciante*

6. *What is and what should never be – Led Zeppelin*

7. *Be Quiet and Drive (Far Away) - Deftones*

8. *Little Wing – Jimi Hendrix*

9. *The Patient - Tool*

10. *Creep– Radiohead*

FIRST LOVE SOUNDTRACK
DISC 2: LANDING

1. *Bird Stealing Bread – Iron & Wine*

2. *Gunner - Denali*

3. *Sour Times – Portishead*

4. *Since I've Been Loving You – Led Zeppelin*

5. *In Circles – Sunny Day Real Estate*

6. *One of My Turns – Pink Floyd*

7. *Suicide Machine – Hum*

8. *Breaking the Broken – Sparta*

9. *Romancing the Italian Horn – Karp/Rye Coalition*

10. *Already Died – Eagles of Death Metal*

is for Genetics

The number of studies on the heritability of anxiety is climbing into the tens of thousands and the overwhelming conclusion of almost all of them is that your susceptibility to anxiety – both as a tempermental tendency and as a clinical disorder – is strongly determined by your genes.

– Scott Stossel, My Age of Anxiety

My maternal great-great-Aunt Clara was admitted to Napa State Hospital[25] in California circa 1960. The original design for this hospital, completed in 1875, included 500 beds. During 1960, the year Clara died within its walls, the population of this stone fortress peaked at more than 5,000 residents.

Clara was diagnosed with "involutional psychotic reaction, melancholia." This disorder was ascribed to peri-and post-menopausal women who developed symptoms of de-

---

25. Formerly, Napa State Asylum before its name change in 1924

pression during their involutional years (40-55 in women). Other common symptoms associated with this diagnosis included marked anxiety, agitation, restlessness, somatic concerns, hypochondria, occasional somatic or nihilistic delusions, insomnia, anorexia, and weight loss.

Psychoanalytically, not much is known about the structure and mechanism of involutional melancholias; they seem to occur in personalities with an outspoken compulsive character of an especially rigid nature. – Otto Fenichel

I've never been hospitalized, but I've experienced symptoms of "involutional psychotic reaction, melancholia" (minus the involutional part): anxiety, restlessness, somatic concerns, hypochondria, and insomnia.

Researchers can't agree on the relevance of the "involutional" part of the diagnosis. This disorder is not listed in the DSM-5, the most recent diagnostic and statistical manual of mental disorders. These days, if a person presented with similar symptoms during their involutional years, they would likely receive a standard depression diagnosis.

Clara never married or had children. Neither did either of the two sisters she lived with in San Francisco prior to her hospitalization. They were all single career women in the 1950s, quite the anomalies at the time.

I don't know why Clara was institutionalized. Family sources believe one of her sisters encouraged it. Did Clara threaten suicide? Was she lashing out at her sisters? I'll never know. Here's what I do know. Clara lived at Napa State Hospital for approximately five months before her death in 1960. Her death certificate indicates acute pneumonia and viral enteritis ("stomach flu") under cause of death. She was only 54 years old when she died.

Remember those *Choose Your Own Adventure* books? Let's follow a similar format to explore possible reasons why Clara died at such a young age. Read option one if you trust a medical record at face value. Skip to option two if you've watched too many episodes of House, M.D. to be satisfied with that approach.

Option 1: Clara died from the conditions listed on her death certificate: acute pneumonia and viral enteritis. The hospital grew overcrowded by the year of her death, and she became afflicted with community-acquired pneumonia in addition to the stomach flu. Her melancholia served as a secondary condition contributing to her death. Her depression contributed to inadequate nutritional intakes. The combination of malnourishment and two infections were adequate to cause death. Symptoms of pneumonia: cough, fatigue, shortness of breath, fever, chest pain, nausea, vomiting, or diarrhea. Symptoms of viral enteritis: fever, nausea, vomiting, diarrhea, abdominal pain.

The fact Clara died from pneumonia at such a young age is noteworthy. Pneumonia is most dangerous in those with an underlying health condition/weakened immune system. Might there have been a different underlying disease wreaking havoc on her body, making her weaker than an average woman of her age?

Clara's niece, my maternal grandmother, visited Clara during the summer of 1957, three years before Clara's hospitalization. My grandmother noticed Clara's eyes had transformed by this time, appearing to bulge out of their sockets. In Clara's youth, her eyes did not present as bulging.

Clara may have suffered from undiagnosed Graves' disease. Graves' disease is an autoimmune hyperthyroid condition which may produce neuropsychiatric symptoms. The more severe the thyroid disease, the more severe the mood changes. Thyroid dysfunction is more common in women and those with a family history. Clara's sister and niece both had severe thyroid issues. Symptoms of Graves' disease: weight loss, rapid heart rate, frequent bowel movements, anxiety and irritability, heat sensitivity, bulging eyes. Hyperthyroidism "...symptoms can be episodic or may develop into mania, depression, and delirium."[26]

Unfortunately, the connection between depression and thyroid dysfunction was not mentioned in the medical literature until 1969, nine years after Clara's death. Did Clara's odd behavior stem from an unruly thyroid in need of treatment?

Option 2: Clara died from an untreated thyroid storm.[27] Symptoms: high fever, rapid heart rate, chest pain, breathing difficulty, dehydration, nausea/vomiting, and diarrhea. Relevant risk factors: untreated hyperthyroidism (Graves' disease), being female, severe emotional stress, and infections, especially pneumonia.

All the other women in Clara's immediate family, including her mother and sisters, died in their 70s. I wonder if Clara would have lived another 20 years if she never lived in an institution. If she received the outpatient care more commonplace during the decade after her death, would her life have been spared?

§

---

26. G. Marian et al.

27. Of course, I can't prove this. This condition is considered extremely rare, and I'm not convinced something this dramatic happened. It's just a wild theory based on the clues I have to work with.

Clara's younger sister, Helen, also struggled with depression as a young woman. She received both inpatient and outpatient care. At times, her depression became so severe she stopped eating and required a feeding tube to acquire necessary calories.

I have one memory of Helen. My family and I went to visit her in North Carolina. We took her to a restaurant for dinner. She didn't wish to eat much, so she ordered a "small salad." When the waiter brought out a heaping bowl full of produce, she laughed and laughed, finding the large proportions humorous.

Several years after Clara's death, Helen was seen at the renowned Mayo Clinic in Rochester, Minnesota where they discovered her thyroid to be dysfunctional. Unfortunately, whatever treatment she received for her thyroid did not erase her mental health issues. The plague of Helen's depression lingered. Her depression was so resistant she received electroshock therapy (ECT) several times throughout her life.

ECT gets a bad rap in horror movies for a reason. When first developed in 1938, the administered voltage caused violent convulsions, leading to broken bones. There is also evidence to suggest the threat of ECT was used by mental hospital staff to control difficult patients.

By the time Clara and Helen would have received ECT,[28] most of the awful initial drawbacks had been fixed. Doctors began to provide muscle relaxants and anesthesia during treatments and reduced the voltage administered.

---

28. I don't have an actual record of the treatments Clara received. These are protected under health privacy laws. ECT was a common treatment for depression at the time, so she likely received it.

ECT resets the brain for a period and serves as an effective option for those with severe depression who don't respond to other treatment methods. But it's not perfect: many people experience after-effects, including headaches and short-term memory loss. In addition, most patients will relapse and need additional treatments throughout their life to return to remission.

§

Having a first-degree relative with an anxiety disorder bumps up a person's risk of developing one up to five times that of the general population. My older sister didn't understand my panic attacks when they first began, but as she got older, she too was afflicted. My younger sister got a tattoo on her fore-arm to reference when her anxiety flares up: a heart monitor symbol leading up to the phrase "I'm okay."

Women are twice as likely to develop an anxiety disorder, and mothers who are stressed during pregnancy are more likely to produce anxious children. My maternal grandmother and both of her daughters, including my mother, struggle with anxiety. I procreated with someone who does not have an anxiety disorder and hoped his genes would override mine, sparing my daughter, Ivy, from my nervous lineage. No dice. She is only 5 years old and has already exhibited anxious behaviors severe enough for me to initiate therapy.

Anxiety disorders are the most common mental illness in the United States. There's a long- running joke on my mom's side of the family that we are "dysfunctional." This may be true, but at least we're in good company.

is for hypochondriacal Tendencies

During my senior year of high school, my boyfriend Romeo cheated on me (for the second time) with his ex-girlfriend. According to the rumors among our mutual friends, she started hanging out with strippers around the same time.

My analysis of the situation:

 Girl hangs out with strippers—> Girl has sex with boy—> Boy has sex with me—>

Would they make a Lifetime movie about me and my tragic struggle with AIDS?

The estimated average risk of Romeo contracting HIV from his (hypothetically infected) ex: approximately 1 out of 2,500.

The estimated average risk of Romeo transmitting that HIV infection to me: approximately 1 out of 1,250.

Statistics rarely comfort me. If something only happens to 1 person out of 1,250, why shouldn't I be the unfortunate recipient?

One morning I awoke, consumed with despair. The idea HIV lurked within my body tugged at my brain. In the dark early hours, I cranked up the heat on the thermostat and sat in front of a wall vent in the living room: an old comfort. When I was in elementary school, I often began school days this way. In my childhood home, I dressed in front of a bathroom space heater or huddled in front of a furnace vent in our family room. Now, I longed to be the human equivalent of a cat curled up by the fireplace, but my senses were heightened in an unpleasant way. The overhead lights appeared more garish than usual. The world had grown more threatening overnight, and nothing could dissolve this pit of terror in my gut.

Nonetheless, I tried to focus during school. I immersed myself in my work, and for a blissful period, my life proceeded as normal. But then the thought would catch me off guard, jolting me back into a hopeless mindset:

Oh yeah. I might die soon.

During art class, I stared at Christopher Guest's *Best in Show* and *A Mighty Wind* posters displayed on the walls around me. Even satirical grins offered no solace.

After school, I walked to a nearby playground. I plopped down on a swing and contemplated my destroyed future. This cheating episode happened months before Romeo confessed. During that time, I lost my virginity to him, oblivious. Romeo and I never used condoms because I took birth control pills. He didn't use protection with *her* either and now, my body had been violated by a person I loved. As I swirled the tips of my green Converse tennis shoes in the sand, I realized only one thing could make this torture stop: insisting Romeo get tested for HIV.

He tested negative. My fear diminished but lingered. I read the sinister virus can take several months to show up on a blood test, and while we were close to the recommended wait time, we had not yet surpassed it. I tried to shoo this feeling from my mind.

§

Starting in the first grade, daily tummy aches led me to the nurse's office on a regular basis. The nurse caught on to my repeat visits. She glanced at me with a skeptical eye and told me to lie down for a bit. I knew I had to be convincing to be sent home, but that was always the goal: get back to my safe place and my parents, the only people who could untangle the knots in my stomach.

One day while sitting in the computer lab, a storm brewed outside. Thunder boomed through the walls, and my heart leapt into my throat. *What if there is a tornado? Will I be okay? Will my family be okay? I gotta get out of here!*

The nurse sent me to the small room attached to her office. I squirmed on the foam pathetic- excuse-for-a mattress, study-ing the large painted brick wall. I found it soothing to be alone in this room, away from the chaos of the classroom. In a mirror hung on the wall, I made goofy faces. (Clearly, suffering). Somehow, the storm psyched me up enough to elicit a mild fever, so I was homeward bound!

Back before we could look up our symptoms online, there were books that connected the dots for us. My family owned a medical book which listed various health conditions with symptom flow charts. It was one of my favorite books. In fact, my mom bought me my own copy as a teenager.[29] Us-ing my index finger, I would trace the line of arrows until settling upon the worst possible conclusion.

---

29. NERD ALERT

As young as 9 years old, I suspected cancer lived in my body. What else could explain this constant stream of unremitting feelings, this overwhelming sense of doom? Often dizzy and nauseated, I could not explain why I felt so off. A dire diagnosis seemed the only reasonable explanation. When I later discovered these strange perceptions were caused by anxiety, I set my cancer self-diagnosis aside.

Toward the end of college, my doctor diagnosed me with asthma. She prescribed an inhaler for me to use, as needed. I didn't trust myself to make that call. I posed this question to my public library supervisor who had dealt with asthma for years:

"How do I know if I need to use my inhaler?"

She looked at me quizzically: "I mean, you'll know if you can't breathe."

Well, thanks to lifelong anxiety, I tend to breathe in a shallow manner. Just add a dash of nervousness and voila: a sensation of perpetual breathlessness and a sneaking suspicion you might keel over at any moment.

I spent that summer terrified. The humidity made my nostrils swell and often when I suspected an asthma attack, it turned out to be anxiety. When I reached for my Albuterol inhaler, my anxiety escalated to a full-blown panic attack because Albuterol is a stimulant and stimulants inspire hyperventilation. I'm so glad I was warned about all of this by a medical professional (JK, I had to figure it out on my own.)

At age 29, when my daughter Ivy was born, my discharge nurse gave me a sheet of instructions with specific symptoms to monitor for. Over the next few weeks, I fretted over every foreign sensation. Due to an infected ingrown hair near my C-section scar, I expected an emerging uterine infection. I called the Ask-a-Nurse line to inquire about some perceived tightness in my legs. *Blood clots?!* A pinched nerve in my neck caused my vision to go blurry. As I struggled to make sense of the WebMD site pulled up on my phone, I worried I might be having a stroke.

Inconclusive results on Ivy's hypothyroidism screen prompted a second blood draw. But I had already diagnosed her on my own. Her little hands and feet were so cold. *Wasn't that a symptom of hypothyroidism?* I tried to prepare myself for the pediatrician's affirmation, for the necessity of lifelong medication. Of course, I stressed myself out over nothing. Ivy's second blood draw came back negative.

A few years ago, the "stomach flu" hit me, and I wondered if I might never recover. In the post-flu haze, my body's vulnerabilities taunted me. My immune system only dealt with a minor virus, and yet, my thoughts drifted toward disability and death. I pondered creating a will.

When COVID-19 hit the United States, I *did* create a will. I also purchased an expensive forehead thermometer and oxygen sensor device, attempting to prepare for the worst. Thankfully, by the time the 'rona came for me, I was fully vaccinated and only experienced mild, short-lived symptoms.

The tiniest health set-back leaves me reeling with an uncertainty I long to destroy. If the medical community discovers a cure for anxiety, I may find myself feeling invincible. In the meantime, I shall demand lab tests and verbal reassurance as evidence I am not actively dying. I must continue to follow the arrows pointing in the direction of the worst-case scenario.

I

is for Intrusive Thoughts

If I keep the kitchen floor clean, no one will die. As long as I clench my fists at odd intervals, then the darkness that's within me won't force me to do anything inappropriately violent or sexual at dinner parties. As long as I keep humming a tune, I won't turn gay. They can't get you if you're singing a song, yeah!

– Maria Bamford, "My Anxiety Song"

Around the age of 8, they arrived out of nowhere. Suddenly, my waking life involved startling intrusive thoughts. The people in my head threatened death: for me, for my family, if I failed to heed their demands. I didn't hear *actual* voices, a possible symptom of schizophrenia. Instead, random menacing thoughts that I believed to be honest warnings, conquered my brain. Even with the underdeveloped logic of a child, the ideas seemed odd. But they scared me, and I didn't dare ignore them.

Their commands included hoarding, air typing (using my fingers to mimic typing on a keyboard,) and shooting a basketball into the hoop a specific number of times. No quitting allowed until I met my quota! Otherwise, chaos was guaranteed to follow. The chaos didn't always have a clear definition, but my need to obey stemmed from an unsettling gut feeling: if I don't do *this* thing, right at *this* time, in exactly *this* way, *something* terrible is going to happen.

These thoughts and behaviors were my own private hell. My only saving grace was my cousin Becca. As a young teen, she aspired to become a psychologist, so she offered me counseling services when I went to visit. I tried to explain my awful feelings to her. "Urges" is what I called them, these unstoppable impulses driven by invisible forces. Becca said she experienced them too. She couldn't erase my anxiety but having an ally who understood helped me feel less alone.

If a psychologist had evaluated me, the clinical definition for my "urges" would have been compulsions. I participated in specific acts out of a desperate need to dissolve my anxiety. Consider a person with obsessive-compulsive disorder who incessantly washes their hands due to germ contamination fears. While the idea behind this example seems to stem from rational thought, compulsions may also appear (as in my case) irrational. In addition, you can have compulsions without an OCD diagnosis. The severity and duration of obsessive thoughts and behaviors are more indicative of the disorder than the mere presence of these components on their own.

Anxiety's core is built upon the reality of uncertainty and the fear of lacking control. "What if" thoughts fuel this unease. *What if I lose my job? What if I go crazy? What if my child gets sick?*

In her book *Can't. Just. Stop.,* Sharon Begley explores the idea of mild compulsions being evident all around us. Some people constantly check their smartphones, because they are afraid of missing out on a social event, career opportunity, or emergency communication. Other people like to clean their homes in a specific manner, feeling it's the one place in the universe where they can maintain some semblance of order. As the author described, finding simple actions that reduce our unease is a wonderful, adaptive response.

Unfortunately, things can spiral out of control for certain individuals thanks to a random mix of genetic and environmental vulnerabilities. The compulsions may become so time-consuming, upsetting, and/or socially stigmatized as to cause chronic distress. This is seemingly where quirkiness ends and mental illness begins, but the line is not always clear.

During my "can't throw anything away" phase, I hoarded used toilet paper. This was not a conscious decision. Something in my brain decided it was necessary and my body followed suit. After peeing at school, I wiped myself and saved the toilet paper as I exited the bathroom stall. I then wrapped the toilet paper in paper towels and secretly stuffed the wad into my bag. I did this for several days (maybe even weeks?) before my parents caught on, and heaps of brown paper towels spilled out of my unzipped backpack. This is a disturbing, yet blatant example of how powerful such thoughts can be. The terror I experienced surpassed any ick factor I could conceive. I was so afraid my family would die, as promised by the big bad brain cells, I didn't think twice about this behavior. It was a small price to pay for saving lives.

A woman with OCD named Shala Nicely says it best in *Can't. Just. Stop:* "It's a hot, sick, molten feeling that grows and expands and fills your whole core with fear. You do whatever *he*[30]says. "He" refers to the puppeteer in her mind.

---

30. Emphasis mine

On one occasion, I experienced an episode while cleaning my room. My parents helped, which created a great deal of stress for me. I wanted to determine which items stayed and which ones got thrown out. Rather, I wanted to allow the (figurative) people in my head to dictate what I needed to hold onto for ensured safety. At some point in the cleaning process, my parents recognized my warped priorities: how *everything* was precious to me. I forbade my parents from throwing away the dust bunnies swept off the floor, the collected lint at the bottom of my drawers.

"Noooooooooooo!" I cried and begged them not to dump the dustpan in the trash.

They exchanged a concerned look but decided it wasn't worth the fight. The remnants were collected in a jar. The next day after a good night's sleep, I regained some sense. Maybe I only needed a nap to view this dirt receptacle as unworthy treasure. I told my parents I was just being silly, and of course we could throw away that dumb jar.

This was my first (self-initiated) dose of exposure therapy, a known effective treatment for anxiety disorders. Exposure therapy is a behavioral approach that encourages a person to resist the actions allowing them to feel safe, so they may observe the lack of consequences. Repeated doses of exposure therapy typically alleviate the associated fears over time. In this instance, I threw away junk I deemed significant, and my parents didn't die as a result. Perhaps the big bad brain cells weren't so smart after all.

I didn't know about exposure therapy at the time. I wouldn't piece together what this phase of my life meant until I took college courses for my psychology minor and completed additional self-study to feed my own curiosity.

My parents didn't understand the psychology behind my behaviors. They both faced anxiety in the past, but my manifestations didn't fit the stereotypical bill. My dad was a nervous child, always assuming the worst when a parent ran late. My mom had panic attacks in her twenties, experiencing shortness of breath and heart palpitations. I collected garbage. Since most of my suffering took place internally, and my parents only caught glimpses of the repercussions, they never sought professional help for me. The '90s were not a prime time for parents to be woke to such things. I was just a quirky kid, right?

These strange behaviors decorated my elementary days. They were thankfully short-lived and died out before middle school. But soon enough, my brain would find other ways of ordering me around.

is for Journal Entries

The following (unedited) excerpts are from journals I kept between the grades of 4 through 6.

> *03/04/1997 – What I really want is to keep heathy by brushing my teeth after every meal, exercising enough to stay fit and heathy, Getting enough sleep, washing my hands a lote to help keep germs away from making me sick, staying clean, eating foods that are heathy, and most of all get rid of my fears and get self-esteem.*

Dreams VS Reality

Brushing my teeth after every meal: I never brushed my teeth after lunch, and I occasionally skipped brushing my teeth before bed.

Exercising enough to stay fit and heathy: Hmm—does leaving the den to grab more Doritos count?

Getting enough sleep: But it's Saturday and Snick is on!

Washing my hands a lot to help keep germs away from making me sick: My paternal grandmother chided me for not washing my hands after using her restroom.

"I don't have to wash my hands at home!"

Staying clean: Hey man, the pressure to try heroin in the fourth grade is *strong.* I'm kidding of course. I don't even know what "staying clean" means. I'm fairly confident I bathed on a regular basis?

Eating foods that are healthy: I ate some canned peaches (in heavy syrup) and a few canned green beans with my microwaved veal patty. Ooh! And I drank a Hi-C juice box which meets 100% of my daily vitamin C needs. Picture. Of. Health.

And most of all, get rid of my fears and get self-esteem: Uff, kid. I don't how to break this to you. You will shed some of your fears as you grow. For example, you will stop worrying about Gremlins under your bed and whether Tyler Johnson *likes* likes you. Unfortunately, these will be replaced by worries pertaining to melting ice caps, America's undying love for assault weapons, and the fact you're responsible for bringing a human into this Godforsaken world.

> *03/06/1997 – Today on the bus I got an ear ache, so I layed down. When we got to school and I got up I was dizzy. So Sam and Kelsey walked me to the nurses office. I went home and felt fine later I think I relized some of it might have been an ear infection, but most of it from panic attach. I think I've been getting panic attachs scared about moving infact i'm positive. I hope we don't move until after the school years done.*

My cousin Becca is my sister from another mister. She was five years older than me and had already experienced several panic attacks by the time they came for me. Becca is the reason I knew what a "panic attach" was, in the year 1997, at the age of 10-years-old.

> *03/07/1997 - This morning again I felt really dizzy and I felt like I was going to faint, so I layed down it was another panic attach, but still I was in bed all morning till in the afternoon I felt fine and I had alote of soda crackers, two glasses of 7up, and a cheese sandwhich for lunch. I didn't have breakfast or dinner because I was nautous. At nights I got it again I was starving and nervous.*
>
> *03/08/1997 - This morning when I woke up guess what I felt dizzy, but only for awhile. I was hungry, but I felt like if I ate anything I would gag, think I was going to puke and would. Then I called Becca and she told me she had the same thing and then she told me some of the foods she felt comfitrobal with. She said apples, soda crackers, toast or chicken noodle soup.[31] I told her an apple was the only thing that sounded good, so when we went into town. Mom bought a bag of apples and doughnuts and I had both and felt better. Right now usually I would be having a panic attach, but i'm doing better now that I know I can call Rebecca whenever I want and she always calms me down. Tonight Jaymie is sleeping over. I'm excited. I hope I don't have another panic attach cause if I don't I'll have a lote of fun i'm pretty sure.*

---

31. Becca was (much later) diagnosed with Celiac disease, an autoimmune condition in which the body attacks its own intestines in response to gluten ingestion. She cringes when she looks at this list of "comfort" foods now.

As far as I can remember, Jaymie and I had a wonderful time.

04/02/1997 – We sold our house and my last day of school is April 3rd and we're moving on April 6th...Sometimes I cry for no reasons because...I want self esteem, I'm a whimp, and i'm not the heathyest person in the world. I don't want panic attacs.

05/08/1998 – I didn't write to you earlier because I didn't, but still don't how to write what happened today to show just how much today hurt. Everything was fine until lunch. I was so nervous that I didn't eat much. When a little while after lunch I didn't feel good, I thought it was because I ate something that made my stomach hurt. The nervousness tenses the muscles in my body, especially my stomach. By the time we were supposed to do the Mothers Day program. I was so nervous ^that I felt I was going to throw up. So Mrs. Poppen told me that I could just sit with my mom. I told my mom I had to go to the bathroom because I wanted to get out of the library. I was crying and embarrassed. I also thought I would try to go to the bathroom. Finally my mom and I decided that I should just go home. Even though my mother and I both knew I was just nervous and having a small panic attack. It is so hard for me to identify my cramps, stomachache, headaches, chills feeling hot, and nasasness from REAL SICK and panic attacks. My mom didn't mind that much about missing the program. But I love my mom so much and I felt gulty for making her come and dress up, and bring her cam-

era just to take me back home. I've cryed
about 9 or S(o?) times seince 12:00 noon to
12:00pm now! I am crying while writing this.
And even though it sounds selfish and feel-
ing sorry for myself I was mad, but actually
just sad because I've worked so hard on this
Mothers Day program for so long and now I
didn't even get to do it. I LOVE MY MOM SO
MUCH & WILL FOREVER. I WANTED TO
SHOW HER THAT!

This is dark comedy gold in my opinion. I can't read this entry without laughing. Perhaps it's cruel to mock this poor 5th grader who "worked so hard" on preparing for a Mother's Day program, but I'm pretty versed at being hard on myself. I love how I thought the only way I could prove my love for my mom was by performing a shitty skit and singing dumb songs in front of a bunch of strangers. I'm sure my mom was *devastated* to miss it.

02/18/1999 – I am under sooo much stress to
be perfect; my parents don't care about me
getting A's in and on everything. Infact, my
mom knows I'm under a lot of pressure, and
she says she wants to see some Bs and Cs
on my next report card. Anyway, homework
is horrible! My daily schedule on weekdays
is…I go to school, I do my homework, I pack
my lunch, I get ready for bed, and I go to bed!

Thank goodness you worked so hard in the 6th grade. St. Cloud State University said it was your middle school transcript that really tipped the balance toward their decision to accept your application for admission—

Please, put that pencil away and go hang out with your friends instead. Do it for me, your Ghost of Christmas Future.

03/07/1999 – I wish I could grow up and grow down. What I mean is I want to grow up, because I hate not being able to stay home alone. I hate being so uncourages and afraid of everything! I also hate not being able to go anywhere without (sister) Lou or mom or dad. And I hate sucking my thumb! That is like being addicted to smoking – you can't stop as long as you try! I also want to grow down, because I am always under so much stress to be a perfectionist & I hate having panic attacks.

It may have been embarrassing to suck your thumb until the age of 13, when shame finally overshadowed your desire for comfort. Sure, stuffing "buddies" [32] into the bottom of your sleeping bag to hide them from your friends during sleepovers = not the proudest moments in your life. But take heart, little one. You never developed a smoking habit.

---

32. I never had an official blankie, but I cycled out pillowcases that my parents referred to as my "buddies."

is for Kindergarten

There is no warning, no prodrome. The onset is as sudden as a car crash. Something in my body or brain has gone dramatically and irrevocably wrong. My noisy internal monologue...coalesces around one certain refrain: I'm dying. I'm dying. I'm dying.

— Andrea Peterson, On Edge

During the fourth grade, my first panic attack invaded as I watched the spooky Disney movie *Watcher in the Woods*. A sudden feeling of doom struck me. *Am I dying?* I started hyperventilating (a term I would soon learn). Invisible fingers clutched tight around my throat.

"I can't breathe!"

My mom recognized my symptoms and grabbed a small paper bag for me to breathe into.[33] Slow and deep, breathe in...

---

33. The logic behind this method: over-breathing leads to low carbon dioxide levels in the blood. Collecting your exhaled CO_2 in a bag and breathing that in helps reset the balance. However, people with lung or heart issues should avoid this method as it may exacerbate certain health conditions.

and out. In…and out. In…and out. The bag crinkled as it expanded, bringing my focus to something other than the scary scene set on pause in the background. The invisible fingers retreated.

My older cousin Becca, who suffered panic attacks as a child, was visiting at the time. She explained these feelings could not actually hurt me. A slight comfort. But after experiencing the horror of this initial attack, my worries over when the next one might hit consumed me.

§

I handled kindergarten well because half-days were still the norm in the early '90s. Our teacher entertained us with books and art projects, and before I knew it, my mom would pick me up for lunch. However, first grade was a hard adjustment. I didn't like being separated from my family for an entire day. I didn't feel secure at school.

My unease reached new heights during the fourth grade. My parents announced we would be moving, leaving our cozy small town of Sabin, Minnesota for the unknown large city of Knoxville, Tennessee. After receiving this daunting news, panic attacks began to disrupt my life.

§

As a troubled 11-year-old, I browsed the self-help section of McKay's, a used bookstore in Knoxville. Bingo! My fingers brushed the spine of a promising title. *From Panic to Power* by Lucinda Bassett became my Bible and my friend. A wave of relief washed over me as I perused the info-packed pages. Like me, this lady worried she might lose control at any moment, felt like she was going crazy. The book described panic disorder as a survival mechanism gone astray in modern times.

During a panic attack, your heart races and blood rushes toward your brain, away from your guts and extremities. This allows your body to tap into all the necessary resources for escaping danger. Cavemen would benefit from such a reaction, should they happen upon a hungry lion. However, for a person with panic disorder, this primal response often occurs outside of any obvious threat.

Your fight-or-flight response may kick in at inappropriate times (such as during a Disney movie) before your conscious brain has a chance to understand whether an actual danger is present. The result? You are bombarded with sudden physical symptoms. Your brain asks, "Why is my heart racing? I feel sick. Is something wrong?" Your anxiety revs up even more, intensifying your experience and perpetuating a cycle of symptoms, fear, and fear of your symptoms.

In April 1999, two years after my family moved to Knoxville, the mass shooting at Columbine High occurred. My classmates and I likely heard a watered-down version of events on Channel One, a news station made for middle school students. I was used to panic attacks seizing me at school over nothing. The last thing I needed was a legitimate reason to worry, but I couldn't escape this new reality. Even in school, the bad guys can get you.

One afternoon, rumors of a bomb threat spread through my middle school. My friends and I didn't understand why our teachers weren't sending us home. We exchanged notes on which my friend Jaimie wrote:

"I'm not kidding we have to get outside. I'm so scared I had a dream last month Before the shooting and I just had Day*sha*vou about that dream,…that dream was of explosions and shooting. My tree died after we planted it on my birthday…When I was born my mom planted a tree and It died 12 days or so afterwards. I'm 12 years old."

My type of logic. Any potential threat (real or imagined) presented as a disastrous nightmare, just waiting to unfold. Sometimes in the thick of fear, we make irrational connections to rationalize our experience. Jaimie's warning provided me with more evidence to trust the sinking feeling in my gut.

I shifted in my seat during math class, unable to concentrate. I can't remember if we confronted our teacher, but if we did, our concerns were ignored. Faculty did not take seriously the rumor tormenting us. I stared at the ticking clock, willing the hands to move faster. The stubborn door refused to reveal whatever shadows might be lurking on the other side. Hiding under my desk would be futile. How quickly this windowless classroom became a tomb.

When school ended, I burst through the outside doors and ran up the hill toward my house, tears streaming down my face. My mom waited at the top of the hill to walk me the rest of the way home.

"There was a bomb threat, and they wouldn't let us leave!"

§

My family moved back to Minnesota before I started junior high. During the seventh or eighth grade, another bomb threat spread through my school. The whole school, staff included, took it seriously. There may have been a difference in the way these threats were received, causing the discrepancy in my experiences, but the details escape me.

The events of that afternoon unsettled me, but I soon moved on. By this time, I had traded my school insecurities for body insecurities. I worried more about what people thought of my appearance than what hid in their lockers. But I was a middle-class white girl, and it was the year 2000. I could afford such luxuries.

§

Have you ever been hypothetically unhinged? I imagined writing a novel centered around a mom who becomes so paralyzed with fear, she transfers her agoraphobia to her daughter. After one too many mornings of listening to school shooting coverage on Minnesota Public Radio, the mom decides to homeschool. Slumber parties become a non-option. What if one of the parents is a child predator? Riding bike around the block is a no-go. Someone could grab her daughter when she turns the corner.

This is a person I could see myself becoming if a few more screws came loose in my head.

Have you ever been hypothetically suicidal? Now that I have my daughter, the idea of existing without her is suffocating. What would happen to me if I lost her to violence? I envision myself driving to the Grand Canyon, numb and robotic in my fog of grief. I take in the brilliant view shortly before a casual step off the cliff. I am sorry for any tourists who must witness this. And most of all for leaving my friends and family in the dust, but she is my one and only baby.

§

In 2020, gun violence became the *number one* leading cause of death in U.S. children. Mass school shootings represent a small fraction of these deaths, but they draw more media attention than other types of campus gun violence: the type children of color experience at much higher rates.

The fear of mass shootings has altered the culture of education in this country. Violent threats lead to classroom lockdowns. More schools use metal detector equipment, and most school districts require active shooter drills. Several states, including Minnesota and Tennessee, have laws in place allowing qualified teachers to carry guns.

April 2019 marked 20 years since the Columbine massacre.

During those two decades, there were 237 school shootings in the U.S. Art reflecting on this phenomenon has infiltrated the mainstream: the movie *Elephant*, the book *We Need to Talk About Kevin,* and Foster the People's eerily catchy tune "Pumped Up Kicks" to name a few examples.

I try to imagine what it must feel like to be a student now. How would I fare with daily reminders of the horrors that might befall my unsuspecting classroom? How would I react to traumatized students on the news begging politicians to do something?

The coronavirus pandemic introduced new terrors to the U.S. educational system, but an increase in remote learning eliminated mass school shootings for an entire year. Is this what it means to look for the silver lining? Yikes. However, as more students return to the classroom, experts predict a return to "normal." In addition, researchers estimate violent crimes will increase over the next several years due to the rising temperatures associated with global warming.

My daughter Ivy will be entering kindergarten soon. As she navigates her school years, I anticipate tough conversations surrounding school violence, and I wonder if I'll be able to find the language. How much worse might the problem become? I shudder to think. When I pack Ivy's lunch for her first day of school, I'll make sure to set aside a paper bag for myself.

is for Loneliness

After watching Forrest Gump around the age of 8, I pined for a relationship like Forrest and Jenny's. I wrote about it in my diary on a regular basis. There was something about a boy taking me seriously, without wanting to make me his girlfriend I yearned for.

I once had a dream about meeting a long-lost elderly aunt who lived in a fancy house and introduced me to a young lad.[34] Somehow in the short duration of a 10-minute dream, an understanding surfaced: this boy and I embodied kindred spirits who insisted on doing everything together, best friends till the end. Upon opening my eyes and realizing this boy was fictitious, a horrible loss settled in my heart.

§

A loneliness enveloped me during my early teens. If my close friends spent time together without me, my self-esteem took a hit. Instead of calling them to make plans, I sat in my room feeling sorry for myself, assuming they didn't want me around.

---

34. *Great Expectations*, anyone?

I often fell asleep with headphones on. I loved to create movies in my mind, syncing up with the notes in my ears. The content ranged from fond memories to fantasies involving kissing whomever I fancied at the time. These boys all seemed as out of reach as my Forrest.

Karl was only slightly older than me but definitely too cool. His shaggy brunette hair and adorable brown eyes enchanted me, but his individuality charmed me the most. He carried around a Simpsons lunchbox, wore mismatching clothes, and stole the school dancefloor with his sick moves and confidence. Karl personified an ideal mix of conventional and unique. He ran on the cross-country team but also roamed the halls doing yo-yo tricks.

I drew a line on my wall, marking his height (for research). I needed to see if I could kiss him on my tiptoes. Even though short women figure out a way to kiss tall men in real life, I remained unaware of such logistics.

As freshmen, my friends and I joked about belonging to the "S.I." (Sexually Inexperienced) Club. If we handed out proper titles, I could have been the president.

Karl heard about the line on my wall through the high school grapevine and (rightly) found it weird. My friend Kelsey teased me about what I'd do next. Measure out his weight in rocks to see if my loft bed could contain both of us? How insulting! I would never do something like *that*.

Brian, another crush I fantasized about, admitted to finding me cute. Unfortunately, I was 15 and he was 20. He lived in the same apartment building as my older cousin, Becca. He was attractive, but I'm sure his most captivating trait was his unattainable nature.

"Age should not matter when it comes to love!" I complained to Becca, wondering why the universe (or culture, at least) forbid Brian and me from being together.

Imagining the two of us in a passionate embrace appeared to be the closest I was going to get. So, I found companionship in my nightly daydreaming while listening to cheesy tunes like "I Could Not Ask For More" by Edwin McCain and "Good Riddance" by Green Day.

§

After I started dating someone during my junior year of high school, I discovered a new brand of loneliness: one that threatened to overwhelm me with its magnitude. While attempting to sleep one night, an emptiness crept in that my boyfriend Romeo filled just hours before.

Earlier in the afternoon, we took a nap together. While spooning on his bed, we listened to the Red Hot Chili Peppers album *By The Way*. I clasped onto Romeo, exuding Ralph Lauren Romance perfume while basking in the scent of his Old Spice deodorant. I finally found my place in the world, and it was carved out in his arms.

I tossed and turned to this mental image. I panicked at the intangible restlessness of not being able to hold him right then. My body ached for his. I didn't want to be with him. I *needed* him. *I shall never again be whole without the presence of another.*

Romeo and I moved to a new city after my high school graduation. We cosigned a lease for an apartment in St. Cloud, Minnesota where I would attend college while Romeo delivered Domino's pizzas. I chose "undeclared" for my major, which mirrored my uncertainty toward any aspect of my life at the time. Nearly 200 miles away from almost everyone we knew, each mile seemed to stretch longer as the days passed.

At school, I made small talk with a few classmates but struggled to connect with people. As an introvert, it often takes me awhile to warm up to others, and the superficial bonding of the college party scene did not appeal to me. So even after a full year of college, no significant friendships transpired. Meanwhile, my soulmate slowly developed a habit of drinking Old English 40s until he turned into a stranger. I spent my days with my nose buried in books, and my evenings avoiding altercations with my transformed roommate.

Sober Romeo named his Telecaster guitar after me, claiming it his other "blonde bombshell." He both flattered and entertained me with his silly sense of humor. Drunk Romeo loved to argue and built mountains out of molehills.

One day after work, he arrived home to find me chatting with our mutual friend Adam, who sat in our living room while I swept the kitchen. After that, Romeo became convinced I intended to leave him for Adam. Having a conversation while sweeping did not fit my definition of an affair but erasing Romeo's delusions proved difficult.

Drunk Romeo relished challenging my beliefs, wringing them dry of any credibility. He listened to Rush Limbaugh on the radio while he delivered pizzas. At night, he'd come home with a new world crisis to discuss, eagerly awaiting my response just so he could contradict it. At 19-years-old, politics did not hold my interest. Based on my general values, I leaned toward the Democratic influence, but I didn't think too much about it. Romeo gave me no choice but to pick a side. Turns out, I fit within the category of "bleeding heart liberal" while Romeo harbored Libertarian ideals.

As Romeo's alcohol consumption increased, so did the corresponding damage: closet doors, my nervous system, and Romeo's pancreas would not go unscathed. Empty bottles and Sparks cans cluttered our living space. Our kitchen overflowed with recyclables. Romeo didn't respond well to criticism. He skipped over the traditional route of agreeing to disagree and instead hurled objects around like a tyrant. He once flung an empty laundry basket by my head, shattering our living room window to show disapproval. Sometimes, exhausted at the concept of another pointless quarrel, I tried to slip away to bed before the liquor filled his veins. He usually noticed, stumbling into the bedroom and turning on the lights, forcing me to engage in conversation.

A poem I wrote during this era of my life features the following line:

I can be alone in heaven or have company in hell.

One night, while finishing a jigsaw puzzle, I said the wrong thing. Romeo kicked the cardboard bearing my meticulous arrangement, scattering 500 pieces around the carpet. I mourned the small remaining semblance of household order, destroyed in an instant.

"I HATE YOU!" Romeo blurted. "FUCK YOU!"

I winced at his words while tears stung my eyes. *Hate? Hate?!* I sobbed on the floor, desperate for my emotional outburst to elicit comfort from Romeo. I needed a hug, reassurance that my overt display of pain had the power to force his arms around my quivering shell. Instead, Drunk Romeo ignored my cries, and my body pulsed with the sensation of abandonment. I was a rhesus monkey, alone in a cage, cuddled up to a terrycloth imposter.

As the demons processed and churned out of his liver, *my* Romeo would resurface.

"You said you hated me!" I pleaded.

"No, I didn't," Romeo said, convinced by his own words.

"Don't you remember?!"

He didn't. And of course, he always apologized—and I always forgave him. He remained my soulmate according to my warped definition, even with his split personality.

I gradually built a backbone as a means of survival. On one occasion, my anger superseded my fear and sorrow. Romeo pitched my navy heirloom chair across the room, the wood cracking like our psyches. I stared at the wreckage, also taking notice of a prized candle holder, fractured down the side from another incident. Sick of flight, I soared straight to fight. I screamed at Romeo, bringing to light the injustice of his actions. Bitter words spilled out of my mouth, the built-up wrath escaping my pores.

Then, the shouting turned to silence. Burning red and breathing hard, I glared at Romeo, as if I'd just won a boxing match. He sat like a zombie on the floor, unresponsive and staring straight ahead, wearing glassy black eyes. Defeat sunk in. He wouldn't remember he broke my furniture. He wouldn't know I stood up for myself. By tomorrow, nothing would be solved. Absolutely nothing.

This boy who taught me how lonely I could feel without someone also showed me how lonely I could feel with a person sitting right beside me. So even while sharing a bed, the theme remained: I spent my nights lying in bed, longing for others.

$\mathcal{M}$
is for Magical Thinking

Throughout my life, I've had numerous flirtations with magical thinking. Some of this has been in line with a normal imagination and cultural rites of passage. For a solid decade, I accepted Santa's ability to travel the entire world in one night, with enough time to read shitty handwritten letters and nosh away on endless chocolate chip cookies.

For approximately two decades, thanks to Disney movies like *The Little Mermaid* and rom coms such as *Never Been Kissed*, I believed romantic love was something that just *happened* to you when you found the "right" person, and this love required minimal effort, because you know—soulmates! And before developing a more cynical worldview, I also used to believe "everything happens for a reason."

When I was younger, I dabbled in superstitions. In the car, I routinely held my breath whenever we drove past a cemetery. I once watched a cartoon cat throw salt over his shoulder while advising, "If you spill the salt, throw it over your shoulder, or you won't live to be much older." That was enough evidence for me. My feet avoided cracks in the sidewalk, seemingly of their own volition. It's nice to know that when my brain was on autopilot, there was a built-in safety net. My mom didn't deserve a broken back due to my carelessness.

During a more abnormal phase, I believed I could make things happen just by thinking about them. My older sister didn't understand when I started having regular panic attacks around the age of 9. Flustered with my irrational behavior, her friend once blurted out:

"If you think you're going to live, you'll live! If you think you're going to die, you will!" which is possibly the *worst* thing you could say to a child in the throes of an anxiety crisis. *What if she's right?* I feared what my mind might conjure up and being responsible for it. Most of all, I worried about death and the horrors it promised.

While watching the Tim Burton film, *The Nightmare Before Christmas*, a sudden wave of terror seized me during the opening song "This Is Halloween." During the lyrics "Everyone hail to the pumpkin song," I closed my eyes and sensed a red tint behind my lids. Did I accidentally bow to these words and promise myself to the devil?! Did this simple act seal my fate of going to hell? The concept haunted me. I searched for a way to undo my assumed damnation, desperate to rid myself of that feeling.

A boy on the school bus told me if you drew a circle around a star and left it by your bed, Satan would visit during the night. After that, I made sure to never draw circles around my stars. And when I said my prayers, I always avoided the one about dying before I wake.

On more than one occasion, I bargained with God. After overindulging in chocolate, I vowed to shun sweets for two whole weeks, if only he'd take pity on me and make the searing stomach pains stop. I offered this deal several times, despite my pathetic success rate. I always allowed my sweet tooth and the rewards of instant gratification to shift my goal date several days earlier.

When my parents failed to pick me up from school or a friend's house on time, I stressed. *My mom said she'd be here five minutes ago! I hope she's okay! What if something is wrong?!* I begged God for my mother's safe arrival, vowing to start reading the Bible every day.

During middle school, my family lived in Tennessee. I strived for academic perfection and spent a depressing amount of time on homework. After grueling over an assignment for hours, I pleaded with God to create some sort of natural disaster. With school canceled, I'd have extra time to complete my work. I offered God the grand prize for this arrangement: I pledged it would prove to me once and for all, he did in fact exist. The next day, school was canceled due to a mild snowstorm. (A snowflake is cause for alarm in the South.) This delighted and impressed me! But my skepticism couldn't help itself from reemerging later in life. Sorry, God. Apparently, I'm not a very loyal person to do business with.

As a teenager, my magical thinking expanded to other realms. *Everything* was a sign. I found meaning in the precise order of license plate letters, in song lyrics on a gifted CD mix, and in astrology definitions. The stars offered further confidence in the chemistry between me and my first love. After all, Capricorns and Virgos make *such* a compatible pair! P-R-O-O-F.

During a junior high sleepover, an Evangelical friend informed me a person must have a "moment" with Jesus, accepting him as their personal savior. The alternative? Be doomed to hell. My Sunday school teacher never warned me! As a Catholic, I simply needed to confess my sins to a priest. He would prescribe a formula based on my indiscretions: x number of Our Fathers, y number of Hail Marys. I followed his directions to realign myself under the good graces of God. At least, this had been my understanding.

Soon after my Evangelical revelation, I lit a candle in my room and promised myself to the Lord. Bowing to Halloween song lyrics, or even embarking on a murderous rampage couldn't threaten my spot in heaven now. I had been saved. Relief coursed through my body as I shoved this huge uncertainty off my plate.

is for Night
(Bears and Scares)

Before possessing adequate language skills, I referred to nightmares as "nightbears." I'd scurry off to my parents' bedroom in a panic, announcing, "I had a nightbear!"

One of my parents would follow me back to my room, lying with me until I fell asleep.

At a young age, I watched the "family friendly"[35] movie *Gremlins*. It haunted me for the duration of my childhood. When bedroom shadows resembled the pointy ears of those gruesome creatures, I burrowed further underneath my covers. Sometimes I rushed around my bedroom floor, picking up all the toys with faces, and hid them under my blankets to protect them. I required reassurance and specific bedtime procedures to feel safe. It didn't help that at the end of *Gremlins*, the voiceover states:

" … turn on all the lights, check all the closets and cup-

---

35. Fun Fact! After Gremlins was released, there was parental backlash against the way the film had been marketed, helping prompt the creation of the PG-13 film rating.

boards, look under all the beds 'cause you never can tell, there just *might be a Gremlin in your house.*"

So I did what any rational person would do and insisted my dad open my closet, show me under the bed, and pop open my dresser drawers while saying, "See? No gremlins."

I occasionally slept in our hallway, sandwiched between my room and my parents' room. Beneath the bright glow of our hall light, my tiny body felt less vulnerable. I could detect hidden creatures beneath my bed and run fewer steps to alert my sleeping parents. The hallway signified the best real estate my folks were willing to offer, preventing their 7-year-old from sleeping in their bed on a habitual basis.

Urban legends also troubled me. Remember the one about the bloody hook on the car door? How about the woman who heard strange noises during the night? She rests her hand over the edge of the bed, reassured when her dog licks her hand. She wakes to a dripping sound, assumed to be a leaky faucet. Instead, she finds her murdered dog, hanging and dripping blood from the shower with a menacing note left on the mirror:

"Humans can lick too!"

In the movie *Urban Legends,* a college girl hears suspicious sounds coming from the other side of her dorm room. She reaches to turn on a lamp, but then changes her mind, deciding her roommate must be getting frisky with a date. In the morning, she wakes to find her roommate slain. On the wall, spelled out in blood:

"Aren't you glad

you didn't turn

on the light?"

You would never catch me with a mouth full of pop rocks and a soda in my hand. But most of all, I took the threat of Bloody Mary very seriously. Summoning a creepy dead woman in front of a mirror was a "game" I refused to support, even on a dare. Mere chanting guaranteed to make her appear. One evening, I sobbed to my dad at bedtime, "What if I say Bloody Mary in my sleep, and I wake up on the other side of the mirror?!"

However, I enjoyed experimenting with other spooky games. For Light as a Feather, Stiff as a Board, one person lies on the floor, and a small group sits, surrounding them. Each person places their outstretched index and middle fingers underneath the body. Then, you repeat "light as a feather, stiff as a board" until the person magically rises into the air! Or at least, that's the idea. It worked well in the teenage witch movie *The Craft*, but my friends and I never mastered levitation. Perhaps our disadvantage stemmed from our lack of sorcery (or Hollywood magic).

My older sister, Louisa, taught me the Cat Scratch game, and it livened up our slumber parties.

"Close your eyes and listen closely," Louisa instructed while rubbing my temples.

She described a horrifying tale: me coming home from school, finding blood everywhere, my parents missing. The story melded into the description of an evil black cat with red eyes and sharp claws. Louisa finished the story with a final shout and emphatic jolt, her fingers still glued to my head, "…it SCRATCHES you!" I lifted the back of my shirt up for all to see: several red scratches etched across my pale white back. We all marveled at the evidence of my foolish mind.

As an adult, I have refined my methods for dealing with late night scares. If I must sleep in a room with a mirror: I remove it, turn it around, or cover it up (if possible). Problem solved! As for fending off those hidden monsters in my bedroom? These days I check my own closets. Instead of gremlins, I find blankets under which a killer *might* be hiding, smart enough to hold their breath so no movement is detected.

Did you know serial killers are watching your every move? For proof, please refer to the urban legends mentioned above. Bad guys know when your partner or roommate is leaving town. This is when they will make their attack, as you are completely helpless on your own. I may have just saved your life, so you're welcome.

§

Several years ago, my husband Derek left for a fishing trip to Lake of the Woods, or wherever selfish boys go when they leave their damsels in distress back at home. I already knew my sleep would be shitty until he returned, so I focused on my main objectives:

1. Distract myself in the early evening with social events, Internet adventures, or Netflix.

2. Survive the night.

Once the sun started setting, I double-checked the locks on my windows and doors. I needed to ensure an uninvited guest wasn't tucked away, so I investigated each nook and cranny of the house. I assumed a murderer would hide within my walls, waiting for me to succumb to a false comfort before heading to bed.[36] *I'm on to you, bad guy.* I rustled through boxes, clothes, anything capable of camouflaging a masked killer in my presence.

---

36. It's possible I watched *When a Stranger Calls Back* one too many times as a teenager.

When I allowed myself to retire for the evening, I took a deep breath and clicked off the lamp beside the bed.

< Creak>

Ah! I scrambled out of bed to turn a light on in a neighboring room, hoping this might deter a person from breaking in. I reluctantly crawled back under the covers.

<Thud!>

Just a car door from down the street, right?! I don't know. That sounded close! My heart thumped violently in my ears, my mind visualizing an attacker creeping closer to my bedroom. I reached over to grab my only hope for survival from my night table: the bear spray from our Glacier National Park camping trip. With the power to take down one of nature's largest beasts, it seemed like a decent replacement for a proper handgun. Locked and loaded, I hyperventilated beneath the covers, praying the nightbears away.

§

After my daughter Ivy was born, I started to feel more comfortable sleeping in the house without Derek. I still checked doors and windows with a careful eye and continued to sleep with mace[37] beside the bed. But having another person in the house (even a baby) helped calm my nighttime nerves...

Until it *didn't.*

Derek left one morning to work on projects at his parents' lake place. He planned to spend the night there, so my toddler and I had the house to ourselves that evening.

Ivy waddled into my bedroom in the early AM hours. Maybe around midnight? I followed her back to her room and fell asleep beside her on the bed.

---

37. The bear spray expired.

<BOOM!>

<CRASH!!>

Sounds nobody wants to hear at four in the morning assaulted my ears. I sat up gasping, trying to figure out what I had heard. First, I wondered if the boom came from my daughter rolling off the bed. In hindsight, the sound was much louder than that. But being ripped out of the dream world in a violent manner is disorienting. My daughter remained fast asleep on the bed.

My mind raced with possibilities. *INTRUDER? GUNSHOT? Maybe something tipped over, creating some unforeseen domino effect. Did the aquarium explode?*

I crept out of Ivy's bedroom and walked to the end of the hallway, listening for clues from the top of the staircase.

Silence.

The mace! After collecting my weapon from the drawer beside my bed, I began my shaky descent down the stairs, one creaky step at a time. From the dim glow peeking through the blinds, I spotted gleaming pieces on the hardwood. *Are my eyes playing tricks on me?*

I turned on the dining room light to find shiny shards of glass scattered across my floor, remnants of a destroyed window. A rogue gunshot? A neighbor with a vendetta? *Who would do this? How? Why?!* I flipped on every light switch on the main floor and dialed 9-1-1.

The dispatcher encouraged me to go back upstairs until the police arrived. I decided to sit on the steps, so I could keep my eyes on the main floor and my ears on the upper level.

Two police officers showed up to survey the scene. One mentioned they had been called to investigate other weird happenings in the area. The other delivered an update on what he discovered outside: a spilled bucket of rotting vegetables amid broken glass. Some creative asshole used our compost bucket to smash our window![38]

After the cops left, the adrenaline still coursing through my veins would not allow sleep. Instead, I swept the sparkling dust off my floor, rearranged furniture, swept the floor again, and fashioned a window band-aid out of paper and cardboard. I willed the sun to rise and posted pictures of the damage on Facebook.

<HISS!>

Is someone lighting fireworks outside my window?!

I jumped for my phone and dialed the cop who told me to call with any further developments. Then, I immediately hung up after discovering the guilty culprit: my paper/cardboard creation had slid off the window.

§

What are the odds of something like that happening again? I will not be defeated by a random act of vandalism!

Just kidding! The last time Derek left town for an extended period, I made plans to stay at my mom's house.

I guess the goddamn gremlins have won.

---

38. I am grateful they didn't use the nearby patio blocks instead, but seriously, what is *wrong* with people?

is for Overachiever

Perfectionism is self-abuse of the highest order.

-Anne Wilson Schaef

<u>Checklist:</u>

Well, I successfully survived another day of the 6th grade! The gorgeous Brook still only thinks of me as a friend (I'm working on him), but Ms. Musser liked the story I wrote about her. All-in-all, it was a good day.

Every day after school, I follow the list below, so I don't forget anything. Anyway, I have SO much to do, so I better get started!

** Eat a Snack:*

I set my backpack down and head to the kitchen. After rummaging through the cupboards, I settle on a bowl of Frosted Flakes. Study fuel!

Pack my lunch for the next day:

I assemble a balanced meal, stuffing all my selections into separate plastic bags: a turkey sandwich on white bread, pretzels, baby carrots, and a banana. As I stuff the food into my bright blue lunch tote, I tuck a dollar bill in the side. The money is for the vending machine at school, so I can have a Snickers bar for dessert! I put my lunch in the refrigerator and head upstairs to my room.

Clean my room:

I enter my room, finding it how I left it: almost perfect. **Almost.** *I walk the perimeter as always: starting to the left of my bed and moving clockwise. I admire my postcards and magazine cut-outs as I press the sticky putty corners of each decoration, ensuring they are fully secure. I gaze fondly at Leonardo's face as I smooth my Titanic poster against the wall. My trinkets along the window need adjusting.* **There we go!** *I nudge my dolphin snow globe slightly, bringing it back to its central alignment. I use a broom to sweep all the fibers of my forest-green rug in one direction.*

"Hey kiddo!" my dad says, walking into my room and landing on top of all my hard work.

"Dad!" I scold him, noticing the lighter green streaks created by the friction of his feet. "I just swept that!"

"Sorry!" he chuckles, stepping aside onto the hardwood panels.

I grab the broom and fix the ruined strands. A slice of sunshine streams through my windows, settles on the rug. This warm spot will soon attract my dog Goldy to come lay down, but I will forgive her. She doesn't know any better, and I can always re-sweep once she leaves. Everything in its right place.

Play with my hamster:

"Hi Angel!"

I scoop her delicate feet into my left palm and pet her silky golden fur with my right. I know she needs daily exercise thanks to a pet guide I checked out from the library. I let Angel scurry around the edges of my closet, guiding her with my hands along our usual path.

Practice my clarinet:

Inside my bedroom, the music constantly starts and stops. Whenever I mess up a note or get the beat wrong, I must start from the beginning.

"You have a phone call, Justine. It's Sarah," my mom announces as she opens my door.

"Tell her I can't talk right now. I'm busy," I reply, cradling my clarinet in the proper finger position, glaring at the stubborn piece of music in front of me.

"Too busy to talk to your friends?" my mom says, raising her eyebrows.

"Yes. I have to practice."

As my mom reluctantly shuts the door in pursuit of the phone, I bring the instrument back up to my mouth and continue my session. Now where was I? Ah yes, back to the top. You know what they say: practice makes perfect!

HOMEWORK:

We have reached the last item on my list and the most important part of my day! Getting A's is essential, even if my parents don't think so. Allow me to explain.

I had to go to the doctor a few weeks ago because I had some strange, itchy bumps below my armpit. It was terribly uncomfortable, so my mom made an appointment.

"It's shingles," the doctor explained. "We don't usually see this in someone so young!"

I guess I got shingles because of stress. My mom told me she wanted to see some B's and C's on my next report card. I nodded, but honestly, I can't do that. I have to be perfect, you see. My parents just don't get it.

So, let's get started with social studies homework. I need to read two chapters and answer the review questions at the end of each chapter.

After reading the first chapter and taking diligent notes, I read the first review question:

1. *A _____ shows identifiable landmarks such as mountains, rivers, lakes, oceans, and other permanent geographic features.*

   A. ***Physical map***

   B. ***Political map***

   C. ***Survey map***

   D. ***Vacation map***

I gather my supplies and ponder the answer. I only like college-lined paper, because wide-ruled doesn't make my handwriting look as neat. I prefer mechanical pencils to regular wooden pencils, because they leave a darker, more definitive mark. Ooh I got it!

I bring the graphite to the page: ***B. Political map***

Oops! I meant A! I press the square white eraser to the page. It looks sloppy now. I need a new piece of paper.

A. Physical map

Ugh! I tried too hard to fix that "p" and now it looks weird. I need a new sheet of paper.

Justine_Cadwell

Period 5

Hmm. I wrote my name in the upper right-hand corner and underlined it, but the line isn't straight. Bring on the next sheet of paper...

This assignment took me two whole hours! I hope I have enough time to finish the rest of my homework by tomorrow. I have SO much to do!

§

During the 7th grade, a recurring geography assignment involved color-coding territorial maps with colored pencils. I once woke my mom up at 2 AM, crying over a ruined attempt. I couldn't get the colors to blend correctly, according to my specifications.

"I need to start over, but I only have one map!"

My mom showed no sympathy. "Why are you still up? It's a school night!"

I couldn't explain my incessant drive to produce a flawless product. I still can't.

§

Researchers have identified two main types of perfectionists. "Normal" perfectionists derive pleasure from their efforts, and their self-esteem is not affected by outcomes. Neurotic perfectionists often set high personal standards, evaluating their self-worth in relation to achievement or failure.

§

During my early college years, I studied every assigned reading with the precision of a lab chemist. I memorized and analyzed as if my life depended on it. Remember that annoying kid who always raised their hand in class and repeatedly made the Dean's list? Yeah, that was me.

I grew accustomed to praise, so when my efforts went unappreciated by one of my employers, it startled my constitution.

Sitting in a booth across from my Subway manager, she stated mid-review:

"Some of the girls have mentioned you take a long time completing tasks you don't want to do." Rage builds in my gut. *Traitors.* "And just now, you were really taking your time."

I replayed the previous 20 minutes in my brain. After my manager arrived at the store, she sent me outside, so she could speak to my coworkers in private. She told me to pick up any trash cluttering our back parking lot. I dutifully obeyed by picking up every cigarette butt in my path. She called me in too soon, forcing me to leave some chip bags and other more obvious debris behind.

"You told me to pick up the litter?" I replied.

My manager scoffed. "*Every* cigarette butt?"

"Yes? You asked me to pick up the litter?"

Doing the job right took precedence over speed. Some of the more obvious debris remained because I started at the top: with the tiny remnants of tobacco paper.

My coworkers betrayed me. I envisioned myself plugging away at work tasks, doing my best while they judged me as lazy. My mind wandered to a recent occasion. One of the girls popped her head in, checking my progress while I re-stocked the chips in the back room. The other workers quick-ly shoved new chips onto the rack, but I made sure to follow the golden rule of FIFO: first in, first out. Each bag of chips was arranged according to their expiration date. I smoothed individual bags and straightened each row of flavors, ensur-ing a neat, orderly display. *Excuse me* if there were other things that needed to get done. *One thing at a time!*

My other job was a work-study position at an art gallery. Ap-plying the same meticulous behavior in this position earned me the nickname: "The Amazing Justine." At least *this* boss appreciated me. With only a sprinkle of customers to assist each day, the pace was slow, providing adequate time to be thorough in all my tasks. I wrote down every piece of infor-mation when somebody left a voicemail, prompting the birth of my fabulous reputation. Data entry was completed with skill. I cleaned out a storage room, carefully separating and organizing all the boxes of old and new art. I typed out art-ist biographies to include with purchases and rewrote price tags in prettier handwriting. My supervisor, a kind and laid-back woman, casually suggested projects to work on, and I pounced on them as if under a deadline.

Whenever a job becomes easy, I create challenges for myself beyond my assigned duties. At Subway, instead of blindly stuffing a customer's sandwich into a bag, I designed social experiments. For small orders, I chose my words carefully, asking customers if they "needed" a bag. I enjoyed watching the wheels turn in their heads. My proudest moments oc-curred when customers replied: "No, I guess not." Maybe I didn't spark an environmental revolution, but at least I saved several plastic bags from circulation, perhaps influencing a few minds in the process. My work mattered, right? *Right?!*

While working at a public library, I tried to become ambi-dextrous, building meaning into menial tasks. I am naturally right-handed, but I used my left hand to fill out repair slips for damaged books. Before adopting this approach, my neat handwriting had been revered and utilized on a regular basis. My coworkers often asked me to write signs for library events. What the staff must have thought, as they watched my esteemed calligraphy turn into chicken scratch. *Did Justine have a stroke? I can hardly read this!*

Outside work, my "leisure" activities tend to have a productive focus as well. I seldom enjoy re-reading books. I rarely watch movies more than once unless I'm watching them with someone else, thereby creating a novel social event. New experiences present themselves as more satisfying, necessary even. Not optimizing my time puts me on edge, as if life is slipping away right under my nose. This might explain why, over the past decade, I have formed a book club, co-hosted a podcast, took bass lessons, sang in a band, embarked on ridiculous diet experiments in the name of science, adopted a plant-based diet, created two blogs, started a YouTube channel, self-taught myself guitar, started writing my own songs, and (finally!) wrote a book. I constantly grapple with the gravity of existential crises, and life is too short to spend it scrolling Facebook.

§

In the book *Too Perfect: When Being in Control Gets Out of Control*, the authors claim perfectionists harbor obsessive personalities, requiring a sense of control to feel safe. Why does this sound familiar? My overachieving behaviors orbit around the itching reality that nothing offers a guarantee. Focusing on specific details allows me to blur the big picture: a 4.0 GPA, endless creative hobbies, and raving job reviews do not matter in the grand scheme of things. I cannot prove my significance through such achievements.

But that's never stopped me from trying.

is for Pain

You can be sure that if 85 percent of fibromyalgia patients were men, rendering them unable to work from extreme fatigue, bone-deep pain, and mind fog—there would be no problem getting the funding and research to look into this scourge upon the modern male workforce.

-*Sarah Ramey,* The Lady's Handbook for Her Mysterious Illness

I wake up stiff as a corpse and silently coin a nickname for myself: "Rig" (short for rigor mortis).

Another night of shallow sleep? Every muscle in my body seized by tension, sends waves of nausea throughout my core. I can tell the brain frogs will descend upon me today. Sorry, I meant brain fog. The value of a task is measured by its energy requirement. I must be careful when delegating my reserves. A few extra chores in the morning might leave me too depleted for a coherent phone conversation that afternoon. Ah yes, just another day in chronic illness paradise.

Research indicates fibromyalgia tends to develop after a triggering circumstance: a car accident, an infection, prolonged stress or emotional trauma. Fibromyalgia has haunted me for nearly 2/3 of my life. My symptoms began near the end of a toxic relationship, as if the torment baton officially passed from my mind to my body. I started experiencing regular bouts of debilitating neck tension and post-exertional malaise: a flu-like response to exercise. In addition, my eyes burned, my chest ached, and pain shot down both my legs. Did I mention the fatigue?

My cousin Becca, a clinical psychologist, had been diagnosed with the same condition a few years before. She verified these seemingly random symptoms could all be connected to one dysfunctional nervous system.

Fibromyalgia is a syndrome characterized by an amplified pain response to normal stimuli. There is no definitive lab test to diagnose fibromyalgia.[39] Various diseases share several of its symptoms, such as multiple sclerosis and Lyme disease. Historically, a fibromyalgia diagnosis depended upon a process of elimination, ruling out illnesses that present with more obvious clinical markers. Now, a diagnosis can be based on symptoms alone. It's also understood fibromyalgia can and often does coexist with other chronic pain disorders, such as rheumatoid arthritis.

Are fibromyalgia symptoms "all in your head?" Some sufferers have faced this accusation by family, friends, or even healthcare professionals. When fibromyalgia patients are diagnosed, they are more likely to have depression or anxiety compared to the general population, but according to a large

---

39. A possible diagnostic blood test for fibromyalgia, known as an FM/a test, may be more widely available soon. However, more clinical trials are needed before it's accepted as an official diagnostic tool.

2015 Dutch study, most people with fibromyalgia do not have mood or anxiety disorders. In 2018, researchers discovered brain inflammation in fibromyalgia patients. So, I guess the naysayers were partially right, just not in the way they thought. It's all in our heads in the sense that our brains are on fire.

Whether excited or scared about an upcoming event, my nervous system fires up, making me more susceptible to a fibromyalgia flare-up. If I am nervous about something, I'll probably sleep poorly. If I'm anxious about hosting, I'll obsessively clean my house. When you mix a lack of sleep and overexertion into a pot of anxiety, it's the perfect recipe for pain.

§

On the show *Community*, the studious Annie eagerly promotes the company Futurza, a "rising star in pharmaceuticals," to her former study group.

"They invented fibromyalgia *and*—the cure for fibromyalgia!"

Bu-dum-tss?

Whenever chronic illness is mocked on TV, my gut lurches. Do I support freedom of speech? Of course. Have I played Cards Against Humanity and laughed at crude jokes? Of course. Maybe I just can't handle a personal attack. It's true my delicate self-esteem is unlikely to survive a comedic roast. But many people with invisible illnesses, such as fibromyalgia, have had their debilitating symptoms doubted or dismissed. So any joke that reinforces this trend stings.

§

Case reports of fibromyalgia symptoms go back centuries, but its acceptance as a "legitimate" illness only recently came to fruition. Some doctors still treat fibromyalgia with skepticism. No definitive lab test? No physical evidence? The dreaded response too many patients receive:

"But you don't look sick."

§

A band of pain erupts from the right side of my neck, clawing toward my right eye, like a pirate hook. I look at my period prediction app. *Yarr! Time to walk the plank. It's shark week!* A day or two before my period, I am greeted with debilitating pain flare-ups. Imagine coming down with the flu (the unvaccinated kind) every 26 days. My intestines adopt an *everybody out* attitude, resulting in diarrhea and vomiting. If I don't eat often enough, the pain-induced nausea intensifies. Recently I opted to take a hot bath with Epsom salts before eating breakfast. This resulted in me dry heaving over the kitchen garbage can as my bread finished toasting.

All signs point to *lay down and curl up into the fetal position.* But this is a trap, because the less active I am, the more my muscles tense up into a stiff mass. I must force myself to eat. I must force myself to engage in minimal light activity, such as housework or a walk around the block.

Sometimes I fantasize about getting a hormonal IUD so I can skip this monthly ritual. But they freak me out. Given my medical history, I'm certain I'll be one of the poor bastards who suffers complications. I guess I'll just look forward to menopause instead? You know, when my vagina dries up like a desert and hot flashes fuel my insomnia—

being a woman is a joke.

§

Between 80-90% of the people who receive a fibromyalgia diagnosis are women. In Maya Dusenbery's book *Doing Harm*, she explores how traditional medicine leaves many female sufferers behind. There is a sinister history rooted in sexism regarding women with unexplained symptoms. Never mind all the things science got wrong along the way. If there's no immediate explanation based on the current medical model, the default is to assume millions of women are bonkers. Remember hysteria?[40]

Most medical research is conducted on men with results extrapolated to women. Conditions which disproportionately affect women are poorly understood because these diseases were banished to the bottom of the priority list long ago. Thanks primarily to the work of patient advocates, more research funds are being allocated to study diseases like fibromyalgia, but we've got a lot of catching up to do.

§

Because fibromyalgia symptoms tend to wax and wane, my disorder has given me a split personality: one day full of ambition and follow-through, the next devoid of vitality and looking for short-cuts. I receive praise for my attention to detail on the days I function at full capacity. On my bad days, I struggle to find the strength to reciprocate a polite smile.

§

New research (2021) has shown that many fibromyalgia symptoms are caused by antibodies that increase the activity of pain-sensing nerves throughout the body. This critical piece of information may lead to fibromyalgia being officially classified as an autoimmune disease: a condition in which a person's immune system starts attacking healthy cells, tissues, and/or organs. Yay! My body really does hate me as much as I've been telling everybody all these years. Are we having fun yet, class?!

§

My illness hovers over me like a funnel cloud.

---

40. At least we got vibrators out of the deal. But let's be real, women would have invented them eventually.

If I walk to the grocery store to buy supplies, will I be too fatigued to entertain later?

Will my upcoming trip be tainted by disabling pain and vomiting caused by said pain?

Today, my lungs don't have the energy to breathe. If I feel this terrible now, how will I function in 20 years?!

When my symptoms intensify, it's impossible to ignore my condition. Sometimes, in between fibro flares, I fall into a beautiful state of denial.

My body reassembled itself back into a functioning unit!

This honeymoon period inevitably ends, but I live for the illusion of a carefree existence.

§

Managing chronic illness is tricky. Traditionally, conventional doctors are trained to dose symptoms rather than search for root causes. Instead of offering lifestyle tips, many are quick to grab their script pads, scribbling down the name of a drug you may or may not have seen advertised on television. Until recently, I avoided prescription medications to treat my fibromyalgia because side effects never seemed like a stellar deal to me. Trade my current discomfort for a different kind? No thanks.

Holistic practitioners are more open-minded, but often *too* reassuring. Many try to sell the notion fibromyalgia can be cured with a targeted approach. I clung to this promise like a newfound religion. I wanted a savior to show me the way.

For a while, I went to a chiropractor on a regular basis. Spinal adjustments seemed to help. Well, sometimes. In the thick of a bad pain flare, I scheduled an appointment, confident an adjustment would alleviate my agony. At the end of the session, my chiropractor announced with self-satisfaction that my spine was in much better alignment. I nodded, helpless. My nerves remained on fire.

§

I have tried various dietary changes. A few years ago, I underwent MRT[41] food sensitivity testing. This approach involves following a personalized anti-inflammatory diet (also known as a LEAP diet) based on a blood test.

According to my MRT results, my immune system *hates* corn and dislikes: caffeine (dark chocolate, tea), capsaicin (spicy deliciousness!), coffee, cow's milk, garbanzo beans, grapefruit, honeydew, leeks, onions, lettuce, raspberries, watermelon, yogurt, yeast (yogurt, mushrooms, beer, etc.), and wheat.

Fantastic news! Most gluten-free breads have milk and/or corn in them, and even minimally processed soups and snacks often contain onion powder. Also, I have IBS and need to limit other foods for digestive reasons. Have I mentioned I eat a plant-based diet for ethical/environmental reasons? I used to love food, but now eating has become a source of stress. Remember the food pills on *The Jetsons* cartoon? If someone could manufacture some vegan/gluten-free/corn-free meal capsules I could gulp down three times a day, that would be great.

I have seen the research on the LEAP diet[42] and have confidence this method has the potential to reduce fibromyalgia symptoms. However, the testing is not cheap, and I break my diet often because, dammit—I gotta live! Also, I'm lazy and do not enjoy cooking. Food sensitivities can change over time. So while the LEAP diet may offer temporary relief,

41. MRT = Mediator Release Test

42. I completed training to become a certified LEAP therapist: a registered dietitian who helps people navigate their MRT results and plan their menus.

new food sensitivities may sprout up later for those with an aberrant immune system. Anyone up for a rousing game of dietary Whac-A-Mole?

§

Exercise is complicated. With this illness you must move your body the correct amount or pay the consequences. I once scheduled a free personal training session at a gym I frequented. I informed the trainer my fibromyalgia created weight-lifting struggles due to chronic neck pain. He did some "research" before my session and told me he had great news! Exercise had the potential to eliminate ALL my pain! *Bullshit.* The trainer condemned coffee as I stared at an open can of Monster Energy drink on his desk. That should have been all the warning I needed.

He led me through a short, yet brutal routine, suspiciously intense given his pep talk advising a slow, moderate approach. He almost tricked me into committing to more sessions. My God, they're relentless salesmen. But before hiring a trainer unfamiliar with rheumatic conditions, the session caught up with me the next day. I experienced debilitating post-exertional malaise for ***over a week***. My insomnia spiked, my hibernating pain reared its ugly head, and my energy took a serious nose-dive.

§

On the show *Raising Hope*, a kid is teased on the school bus for having an overweight mom. His response? "She can't exercise, because she has fibromyalgia."

Ba-dum-tss?

§

This quest for wellness has left me disheartened. Trying to piece together the magic combination of interventions has cost me more money, patience, and emotional distress than I care to acknowledge.

I used to see a naturopath whose treatment plan helped reduce my symptoms, but the office visits and endless supplements became too costly to maintain. I dream of permanent remission and continue to search for strategies to achieve this as time and finances allow.

There are hopeful avenues I can further explore. Emerging research on new potential treatments include low-dose Naltrexone (touted as a drug option with minimal side effects),[43] EMDR[44] (a psychotherapeutic approach to repairing mental trauma) and neural retraining systems, such as the $400 Gupta meditation program I purchased a couple years ago (and have failed to follow consistently).

I believe my physical ailment was born of stress. Perhaps the chronic stress of anxiety and depression, possibly the acute stress of my damaging relationship, but likely a combination of the two. Whether or not this can be reversed remains to be seen. Due to my inherent perfectionism and hypervigilant nature, living in a heightened state became my cellular blueprint from a young age. My nervous system rewired itself to be hypersensitive. For years, I told my body to constantly be on guard.

Unfortunately for me, it listened.

---

43. I am currently taking this and *think* it's helping.

44. Eye Movement Desensitization and Reprocessing

is for Quicksand

My panic shifts shape each time it appears: sometimes a fist clutched around my windpipe... neck and back needled in electric tension, guts dissolving into liquid or a ratatat heartbeat that shocks me out of sleep and leaves me there, awake, no matter how rude the hour.

– *Kat Kinsman,* Hi, Anxiety

My thoughts are quicksand. I trudge along innocent terrain, then suddenly find myself slipping down, down, down.

I feel normal: bored with winter, but reasonably content. Minimal anxiety...

Then I vomit several times and start to feel weak.

Text to nurse friend, Amber: I am fairly confident I have food poisoning...do I need to worry about replacing electrolytes or can I just drink water?"

I remember a documentary in which they point out how bulimia can be more dangerous than anorexia in the short term due to electrolyte imbalances. Even in the absence of an eating disorder, I worry my sudden vomiting might be enough to create a similar crisis in my own body. I can hardly drink water. My husband Derek makes me a homemade electrolyte drink containing sugar, baking soda, and salt. It's vile.

Drinking it might make me throw-up more.

I could die from an electrolyte imbalance.

Text to Amber: I am bleeding out of my butt. I want it to be funny, but it's not. It [Mayo clinic website] says to "call a provider." Do I need to go to the ER?

Severe cases of food poisoning can cause this! What would we do about our sleeping baby upstairs? She can't come to the ER with us.

What if I am hospitalized and I have to be away from her? I can't breastfeed in the hospital. She'll cry herself to sleep.

Oh wait...

I guess I just got my period.

My appetite remained poor for several days. My assumed food poisoning turned out to be the "stomach flu."

What if I never have an appetite again?

What if I'm not making enough breast milk? I need more calories.

After a few days of forcing down soda crackers and jars of baby food, my appetite resurfaces. I decide to try a substantial meal. I eat a veggie sandwich, a bag of chips, and a cookie. I wash it all down with a lemonade iced tea mix. The blood sugar rush leaves me jittery and nauseated.

Could I have refeeding syndrome?

<Online search>...

Refeeding is the process of re-introducing food after malnourishment or starvation. Refeeding syndrome is a serious

*and potentially **fatal** condition that can occur during refeeding. It's caused by sudden shifts in the electrolytes that help
your body metabolize food. Refeeding syndrome **can affect
anyone**. However, it typically follows a period of: malnourishment, fasting, extreme dieting, famine, starvation.*[45]-

It can be FATAL. It can affect ANYONE.

I have to pick up Ivy.[46]

*I might need to throw-up on the way there...or worse! on the
way back with Ivy in the car...*

§

*My in-laws can tell I'm being weird. I'm trying to be "nor-
mal."*

Act normal. Be normal.

Act normal. Be normal.

Fake it 'til you make it.

Back at home, I tremble on my bed while Ivy looks at books.
She crawls on me, demanding my attention. I don't have any
to spare, my focus set on staying conscious and keeping the
contents of my stomach where they belong. To distract her,
I lead Ivy to a toy shelf in our hallway. I'm trying to make
my way downstairs, but I'm too paralyzed with fear, as if a
hungry lion with bloody jaws is guarding the steps. Ignore
the lion. (Lion's still there!) Face the lion. I'm not afraid of
you! He's not buying it. (No one is.)

Stack these blocks. Say "mhm" to Ivy's babbles, hoping the
lion will spare her. I can't tell if she knows how scary he is,
but she sees him and is trying to figure out how to respond,
searching my face for clues.

---

45. Vandergriendt, healthline article

46. My toddler, from her grandparents' house

143

Ivy knows—

I'm trying to put on a poker face, but she can tell I'm different and it's upsetting her.

I'm a bad mom.

Ivy scampers off to the bathroom and plays with the screw covers on our toilet base.

I need to wash her hands, but I'm too weak to lift her and what if the movement makes me throw-up?

I'm an incompetent mom.

What if I have a nervous breakdown? Derek might leave. I might not be able to take care of Ivy.

I'm a bad wife.

What if I never get better or come down with something serious like cancer where I can't take care of my baby?

What if it ruins her for life?

What if I passed my anxiety on to her?

I have no business being a parent. What was I thinking? I love her so much, and she deserves stability and to be taken care of.

I have no backbone. Normal people just move on from illness.

How will I handle grief someday? If a bout of stomach flu is enough to throw me off balance, what happens when life gets truly difficult?!

My blood turns cold, like somebody changed the faucet position in my body. I tell myself to *breathe*. I tell myself to *relax*. I tell myself to *"play dead."* Instead, my psyche tries to reason with the lion. *Please spare this child!* But the lion does not care. He's hungry and lacks the scruples to give a shit.

What if I throw-up or pass out while Ivy is home? I've never passed out before, but it's never too late to start. I can't put her in her crib or pack-and-play. She'll scream and cry. She'll be confused.

What if she gets into something while my head is in the toilet? She might even reach into it when I come up for air!

I finally make it to my phone on the main floor. Derek is running late.

Text to Derek: On your way?

…

Text from Derek: No, still at work

FUCK!

Text to Derek: Please come home as soon as you can. ~~There's a hungry lion in the stairwell!!~~ I'm not feeling well and need help with the kiddo.

Her screaming is not making the lion any less interested in harassing me.

Derek walks in the door and my shoulders release, my muscles breathing a sigh of relief. The lion tamer is home! Instead of telling him I've been having a panic attack for an hour, I allude to feeling off.

"I think I ate too much too soon. Oh yeah, Ivy was playing with the toilet screw covers again," I say.

"Did you wash her hands before feeding her?" Derek asks.

"Uh—no"

"What the hell?"

I'm a bad mom. I'm an incompetent mom.

§

I make a lot of jokes about having anxiety and depression. It lightens the load. It's a coping mechanism. Unfortunately, when you are in the clutches of an actual panic attack or trapped in the gray gloom of depression, it's No. Fucking. Joke.

When I say fear paralyzed me, as if a lion meant to eat my daughter and me for dinner, I *wish* I was joking. My alarm system takes off at the speed of light. I (sort of) know I'm not dying, but I can't convince the primal part of my brain. Those cells take the form of an aggressive detective, torturing me:

<u>Detective:</u> Are you sure you're not dying?

<u>Rational part of the brain:</u> *Well yeah—I think so.*

<u>Detective:</u> THINK so?! Well that's not very convincing! Do you have any evidence of this?

<u>Rational part of the brain:</u> *Uh—*

(Racing pulse, clammy hands, breathless, light-headed, nauseated)

No?

<u>Detective:</u> So, it sounds to me like you COULD be dying after all. Admit it! You're dying!

<u>Rational part of the brain:</u> *Oh my God! Maybe I am dying!!!*

<u>Detective:</u> So you confess!!

Sometimes I try to console myself with the idea that no matter how terrible things get, writing will be there. Horrible experiences = good writing material. But you know what? Fuck being a tortured artist. I choose calm seas, dammit. I'm too old to romanticize such things. I have things to do and people to take care of.

I'm responsible for another human, and it's terrifying to acknowledge how much my failing body and/or mind might let her down. It leaves a sick feeling in the pit of my stomach. My only hope is getting pulled out of the quicksand before I suffocate—or before that lion eats me while I struggle to get out.

is for Religion

My mother believes a method in the stars dictates who we are and how we ought to live our lives. She is a fallen Catholic and a passionate Sagittarius. When her father died suddenly at the age of 56, grief fractured her trust in God. When my parents divorced and Catholic tradition insisted their marriage be annulled, she refused. As countless victims of predatory priests came forward, and the Catholic Church was charged with covering up decades of abuse, she distanced herself further from the religion in which she was raised. Bible passages and marriage licenses ceased to bring her comfort. Now, she finds relevance in horoscope readings and prefers to sign contracts outside of Mercury Retrograde.

My father believes a deity created the stars above us and weaves meaning into our everyday existence. When I feel overwhelmed by the ugliness of the Christian Right, I must reframe religion through my father's eyes to remember its merits: ritual, community, security, and purpose, with an overall emphasis on love. When my stepmom was diagnosed with leukemia, faith strengthened her and my father's ability to withstand the physical and emotional burden of that reality. Church friends lent their ears to vented sorrows and frustrations, delivered home-cooked meals, and offered their homes as places of respite between treatments.

My husband believes in preparing for a zombie apocalypse. I can never tell if he's serious about the zombie part. For years, I rolled my eyes when he insisted we gather supplies and stock canned goods. But I conceded when my daughter was born three days after Donald Trump won the 2016 U.S. presidential election. We now have a basement shelf that is well-stocked with non-perishable food items as well as a bugout bag full of matches, a water purifying straw, a crank radio, and other Mad Max essentials.

§

As a child, I attended Catholic mass with my family. I frequented Sunday School where one teacher ruined my childhood by claiming animals don't have souls. She must have been too old and jaded to know that *all* dogs go to heaven. Disney had already promised me this, and I intended to reunite with my dog Goldy in heaven one day.

My favorite thing about church was the crispy chocolate chip cookies and neon orange Tang waiting for me after the service. These invoked feelings of pleasure (read: sinful), but I could confess my gluttony to a priest later. I remember reading a book that used a cookie metaphor to explain why I should love God more than my parents. When my parents made cookies, I didn't love the cookies as much as my parents, right? Then I should love God more than my parents because *he* made them! Uh, yeah— nice try. Sorry, but this sounds dumb even to an 8-year-old cookie fiend. No amount of indoctrination could make me love a faceless master creator more than the people who literally wrapped their arms around me on a regular basis.

§

Mostly out of convenience, I considered myself a Christian until mid-college. I had never taken the time to question my religious identity. I liked the idea of prayer. It gave me a way to feel heard and more important, safe.

My friend Kaitlin, a philosophy major, invited me to attend the Science, Religion, and Lunch Seminar series held on our North Dakota State University campus. One speaker introduced a simple concept that presented itself as a revelation to me: if born in a different region, wouldn't I believe the dominant religion taught in that area was *the* one religion to rule them all?

Kaitlin was a self-proclaimed atheist. I couldn't commit to that term because it seemed too definitive. The idea that all earthly interactions were the product of mere coincidence left me sad, scared, and empty. Kaitlin argued how freeing the concept could be, but it would take a few years of inquiry and reflection for me to relate to that view.

I still don't consider myself an atheist. How can you prove there *isn't* anything any more than you can prove there is? I label myself Cathnostic: baptized as a Catholic baby, confirmed agnostic in my adult mind. I assume (and hope) the afterlife consists of nothing but dirt. Frankly, the idea of eternal life sounds exhausting and terrifying to me.

I *am* intrigued by weird proclamations surrounding death, such as the notion that a soul weighs 21 grams based on one scientifically flawed experiment from over a century ago. I find recounted tales of near-death experiences involving bright lights fascinating but suspect the visions are brought forth by a dying brain. I also *kind of* believe in ghosts, in the sense that I love the idea of them and want them to exist. And if energy cannot be created or destroyed, where does it go when we die?

You want a physicist to speak at your funeral. And at one point you'd hope that the physicist would step down from the pulpit and walk to your brokenhearted spouse... and tell him that all the photons that ever bounced off your face, all the particles whose paths were interrupted by your smile, by the touch of your hair, hundreds of trillions of particles, have raced off like children, their ways forever changed by you...According to the law of the conservation of energy, not a bit of you is gone; you're just less orderly

- Aaron Freeman, "All Things Considered"
commentator

§

Religion doesn't inspire me, but science, love, and nature do. I believe in the power of empathy, the necessity of kindness, and the urgency of climate change. At my core, I am a pragmatist (typical Capricorn). As such, I understand the allure of a definitive template, so I've made this one:

1. Thou shalt be kind.

2. Thou shalt vote with thy dollar, supporting companies that give a damn about living beings and this planet.

3. Thou shalt vote with thy pen, supporting candidates who give a damn about living beings and this planet.

4. Thou shalt not impede initiatives to educate women and provide access to birth control.

5. Thou shalt strive toward veganism: the best diet for reducing thy carbon footprint and unnecessary animal suffering.

6. Thou shalt carpool, use public transportation, and walk/bike more often.

7. Thou shalt reduce, reuse, and recycle (in that order).

8. Thou shalt switch to cruelty-free, eco-friendly cleaning/personal care products.

9. Thou shalt waste as little food, water, and electricity as possible.

10. Thou shalt embrace clean energy alternatives.

(On my worst days) Existential dread consumes my belief in my ability to make a difference. I tune out the world and decide it's time for others to pick up the slack. I wholeheartedly believe this planet is doomed, or at least, the humans who inhabit it will soon be extinct. *We deserve this.*

(On my bad days) I focus on my own pathetic struggles. I don't *want* to cook dinner. I don't *want* to load the dishwasher again today. Or ever again in my life. I am lucky to dread these things. I have food to cook and clean water to wash dishes. I even have a machine to do the work for me, giving me more free time than those who must scrub their dishes (if they own any) by hand. I need to believe writing about my privilege will help others recognize theirs, even on their bad days.

(On my good days) I believe in the power of the individual. I need to believe walking, in lieu of driving, to the store, and voting with my dollar is putting a dent in this clusterfuck of a climate dilemma. I need to believe there are enough other individuals out there fighting the good fight to make an impact.

(On my best days) I reach out to others who are hurting, donate my time and/or money. I see progress and trust its trajectory. The brilliance of the human spirit overwhelms me. I feel loved and so, so grateful.

§

My dad invites me to attend church with him, though he knows where I stand. My mom warns me when the planets create obstacles for my Capricorn sign, sometimes with the preface: "Now I know you don't really believe this stuff..." My loved ones are amazing. We hold our own beliefs but allow each other to take comfort in different ideologies. Whatever force is responsible for this acceptance makes life worth living, however we define it.

is for Substance Use

Think for yourself. Question authority.

– Timothy Leary

D.A.R.E. is a program taught to school-age children across the United States. The initials in its name stand for Drug Abuse Resistance Education. During the fifth grade, in the mid-90s, I won a ribbon for writing the best D.A.R.E. essay in the class. For several years, this award made me proud, earning a coveted location in my keepsake box. These days, I display it in my home bar as an ironic symbol.

§

I used to do drugs. I still do, but I used to, too.
– Mitch Hedberg

My boyfriend Romeo dropped out of high school before his junior year. While I spent my afternoons learning algebra, he mastered the ability to stretch time and explore the spaces in his brain. He gladly shared this knowledge with me. The endorphin rushes provided a welcome distraction from perpetual boredom. They made my world appear as dramatic as

I craved it to be.

I had a roof over my head, an overactive mind, and several free hours to kill. Enter: drugs.

§

Weed: Before Romeo and I started dating, I tried smoking weed on several occasions. I exerted minimal inhalation effort, afraid to feel its effects. The first time I inhaled correctly, I was in my room with my friend Annika. I insisted the weed must be laced with something. I felt *weird*.

"No, Justine. You're just high," Annika said.

We invited some guy friends over to hang out. In the meantime, we lost ourselves in the experience. Annika and I stripped down to our undergarments and danced around, emulating a scene from a teen movie.

Knock, knock, knock

Oh my God! They're here! Annika and I shrieked with laughter, scrambling to put on our clothes as quickly as possible.

Knock, knock, knock

"Let us in! What are you guys doing in there?"

I laughed so hard I peed my pants while struggling to pull them up. Annika cackled harder. More urine streamed down my bare legs. Now, my mom chimed in from the other side of the door.

"Justine, what's going on?!"

I was right to have been wary about getting high. It was Out. Of. Control. I told my mom to send the boys away.

After our confused guests left, my mom demanded an explanation. I told myself to *be cool*. But honestly, her glare combined with my altered state? I giggled to myself, avoiding eye contact while spewing out some pathetic story. Needless to say, Annika and I were caught red-handed.

§

Did you know that with enough imagination, several house-hold items can be altered into pipes? Apples, aluminum cans, and plastic shelf posts all serve as decent substitutes until you are old enough to purchase legitimate paraphernalia.

Romeo and I spent a significant portion of our time together in an herbal haze. After taking hits (out of a plastic shelf post) in his bedroom, we exhaled into an empty paper towel roll with scented dryer sheets held over the opposite end. We watched *Most Extreme Elimination Challenge,* a mock Japanese game show where people toppled over obstacles. Might I pass out, or die, from the inability to stop laughing?

Later, I drove home to (hopefully) meet my curfew. By this time, I was better at acting normal while under the influence. My mom only accused me of being stoned when I was sober—which is telling of my inherent nature.

My mom watches TV in the living room as I open our front door.

"How was your night?" my mom asks, glancing in my direction while sprawled out on the couch. The only light in the room streams from the dim glow of the television, padding my confidence to pass the good daughter test. If my eyes were red, she wouldn't be able to tell in this environment.

"Fine," I reply without embellishment, breezing right past her into the kitchen. She did not follow me. Operation *act normal* accomplished.

I pour myself a bowl of generic Cinnamon Toast Crunch. *God, why have I never noticed how delicious this cereal is before? Maybe one more bowl...*With a belly full of carbs, I surrender to slumber.

§

Several years ago, I watched the 1936 film *Reefer Madness* with my husband Derek and his friend. The movie was financed by a church group and created for parents to watch, so they could warn their children about the perils of marijuana. Now it exists as a comedic cult classic.

We laughed and cringed our way through the dramatic scenes. What begins as a fun party with jazz, dancing, and (gasp) some marijuana quickly escalates to scenes involving attempted rape, a woman shot to death, and other good old-fashioned *madness* seemingly inspired by smoking this wild, unpredictable herb.

My daily love affair with weed, the stereotypical "gateway drug"[47] ended long ago, but I whole-heartedly support the legalization of marijuana in all states for both medicinal and recreational use.

You'll never convince me weed is more menacing than alcohol. The concept is laughable and another example of a culture with backward priorities. Too often in this country, stigma outweighs common sense.

Allow the following quiz to illustrate my point:

1. **Which one of these activities is more likely to cause bodily harm?**

a) Watching *Planet Earth* on HDTV while pleasantly sedated in the comfort of your own home

b) Falling off your bike as you try to climb your drunk ass onto it outside a bar

(Not that I've done either of those things...)

2. **Which one of these activities is more dangerous?**

---

47. To be clear, *my* gateway drug, like most teenagers, was alcohol.

a) Hanging out with an ex while under the influence of marijuana, rendering you mute as you stare past each other into an episode of *Aqua Teen Hunger Force*

b) Hanging out with an ex while under the influence of Fireball whisky, creating a blind nostalgia as you stare into each other's eyes across a booth.

(Again, these are just examples.)

My dear friend Katie suffers from trigeminal neuralgia, a rare condition that causes *excruciating* facial pain. She was advised to undergo brain surgery, a procedure called endoscopic vascular decompression, which was expected to help. It didn't. According to Katie:

Due to [the surgery] being unsuccessful, it's been determined I have atypical facial pain which leads most doctors to throw their hands up and tell me they've got no ideas... they don't know what causes it or how to help it, just that it'll progressively get worse, and I'll continue to build a tolerance to the pain meds.

Most medications do not work for Katie. Out of desperation, she manages her pain by popping more pills than any liver should be expected to process.

The biggest statement my neurologist has said that's resonated with me recently is, 'Well the next step would be Fentanyl and good luck finding someone to prescribe you that.' So I'm not going to lie, at this point my resolve is at nil, my hopelessness is at max, and I'm just waiting for a way out.

Katie lives in North Dakota, a state which legalized medical marijuana in 2016. Despite this illusionary success, there was still too much red tape in place for the law to be of any use for several years. Until 2019, the state had yet to dictate which conditions were eligible.

I miss smoking [pot] not only for the pain relief, but also for the relief from focusing on the pain for a while.

Even though the psychoactive ingredient in cannabis has shown promise in alleviating the life-shattering pain Katie deals with daily, it was not an option for her until recently. If she had obtained marijuana illegally, she would have risked losing her job in addition to criminal penalties.

This is the part where you realize how silly/detrimental it is for marijuana to be illegal or inaccessible (despite laws!) in any state. This is the part where you phone your legislators and show up to vote and encourage your friends and family to do the same. This is the part where Katie and I and everyone else who suffers or watches their loved ones suffer unnecessarily thanks you.

§

Friends around me snorted Adderall but I didn't like the idea of anything going up my nose. I generally steered clear of stimulants, knowing the rhythm of my fluttering chest would become my sole focus. Considering how one cup of coffee leaves me trembling and frazzled, cocaine seemed like a death wish. I envisioned myself calling 9-1-1 after snorting a line of coke, gasping to the dispatcher about the pressure surrounding my heart, certain it would stop beating at any moment. Also— "I'm sorry and please help!"

§

Telling teens not to do drugs is about as effective as telling them not to have sex. The bulk of evidence does not support abstinence-only sex education as an effective means of preventing sexual activity. In addition, a sinister side effect of these programs is teens less inclined to use protection, because they weren't taught about the importance of its use or guidance on how to use it. The tough zero-tolerance focus of D.A.R.E. appears to follow a similar success-rate trajectory.

§

Mushrooms: My preference for control saved me from diving too deep into any glorious elixir. I ate just enough mushrooms to see waves in the pavement and vibrant colors in my periphery but not enough to get lost inside these sensations and have a reality crisis.

Romeo played guitar (of course) and his friend Kent drummed. We often went to Kent's house, so they could jam out. I liked to shout out requests and nosh on Arby's roast beef sandwiches while they played gems such as Rage Against the Machine's "Freedom."

On one of these occasions, I strolled my subconscious on mushrooms. For a brief while, the boys wailed out creepy circus music to mess with me. I lied on the floor and studied the colorful Christmas lights fastened to Romeo's amp. The bulbs danced as the notes burst out of the speaker. At times, no other thoughts clouded my experience. Only lights. And music.

For me, mindfulness comes naturally with psychedelics. I think that's part of the allure of "losing your mind." Sometimes, for an over-analytical person, that's just what the doctor ordered.

Everyone should read *How to Change Your Mind: What the New Science of Psychedelics Teaches Us About Consciousness, Dying, Addiction, Depression, and Transcendence* by Michael Pollan. In this book, Pollan outlines how recent studies have shown promise in psilocybin's ability to improve the mental health of terminally ill cancer patients, alleviate depression, and help those with addictions such as alcoholism.

Psilocybin is broken down into psilocin, which stimulates the brain's serotonin receptors. These are the same receptors stimulated by many pharmaceutical anti-depressants, specifically SSRIs. But that's not the type of shit they teach you in D.A.R.E.[48]

§

There will always be kids like me: curious souls undeterred by fear-mongering campaigns that undermine budding intelligence and itching defiance. Teens in this country would be better served by replacing programs focused primarily on restriction with those offering an honest discussion of the risks with additional information on harm reduction.

A new program called "Safety First: Real Drug Education for Teens," designed by Drug Policy Alliance,[49] aims to do exactly that. Created in 2015, this program offers the caveat D.A.R.E. is missing: *if*. Instead of telling kids to "just say no," this approach acknowledges some kids will make the decision to experiment with drugs and provides tips for doing so in the safest way possible. *If* you decide to try a drug: make sure you are in a safe location with people you trust, don't mix different substances, and start with a small dose.

This Safety First curriculum was originally tested as a pilot program in a Manhatten high school. In the Spring of 2019, five San Francisco schools joined the evaluation. One of the highlights of this approach is increased student awareness of how to respond to a drug overdose.

§

---

48. Psychedelics increase entropy in the brain, potentially creating a beneficial environment for people with mental health conditions that include an obsessive/rumination element (OCD, depression, anxiety). However, they may not be appropriate for people with schizophrenia or a history of psychosis. Approach with caution if you suffer from one of these conditions.

49. From BuzzFeedNews article: "Advocacy group that supports medical treatment over criminal penalties for drugs and the legalization of marijuana."

DXM: I read about DXM on Erowid.org.[50] Dextromethorphan (DXM) is an active ingredient found in over-the-counter cough suppressants. If taken in high enough doses, DXM can act as a dissociative.[51]

Romeo was an expert user. A local grocery chain banned him for stuffing cough syrup bottles into his coat pockets. Friends told me stories about the possible plateaus of intoxication. I decided to give in to my curiosities.

I swallowed handfuls of red Robitussen capsules, with Romeo as my guide.

First, the queasiness settled in. Romeo put large headphones over my ears and cranked up Jimi Hendrix. A rollercoaster anticipation took hold, my stomach dropping with that familiar escalation of terror. I tore the headphones off, and Romeo cradled me as I hyperventilated. Was this drug going to kill me or was I having a panic attack? Regardless, the fear of dying dissipated within his embrace. I accepted death, if only in his arms.

Eventually, the anxiety melted into fascination. My body itched relentlessly, then transformed into gelatin. It seemed possible to fold myself into any mold I desired. My brain rested on a distant planet but somehow transmitted words to my mouth that were witty as hell. My eyes faced forward, but I sensed them flitting around in seizure. Time existed only as an abstract concept. A few minutes lasted hours.

Romeo and I kept a DXM journal, writing random nonsensical thoughts about soup flavors and the shape of the sun. A true masterpiece, I assure you.

§

---

50. From the official website: "Erowid is a member-supported organization providing access to reliable, non-judgmental information about psychoactive plants, chemicals, and related issues."

51. Another example of a dissociative drug is PCP.

I don't wish to minimize the horrors some illegal (and prescription) drugs elicit. Many of the people I associated with during my rebellious high school years did not have the luxury of walking away from drug experimentation without a struggle. Some of them still haven't and possibly never will.

§

Alcohol: 99 Blackberries: the quickest route to erasing inhibitions we could get our hands on. Skyy vodka: I locked my bedroom door, played strip poker with Romeo. Black Velvet whisky: A party at my friend Jake's house. I kept a tally on my arm. 5, no 6 shots? Hand me that pen. Southern Comfort: In my backyard, laughing and jumping on the trampoline with Romeo and his friend Ike. Taking shots straight from the bottle on a walk around Oak Grove Park. The warm fluid breathing fire down my esophagus, spreading to my chest. A clear empty bottle between the three of us. The first time I witnessed Romeo's eyes disappear under the influence. Ike on the ground after Romeo pushed him in anger. Fear.

§

Using the word "crisis" to describe the current state of the opioid epidemic is not hyperbolic. In 2018, opiate overdose stood as the leading cause of death in Americans under 50 years old. But to lump all illegal drugs under one scary umbrella is ridiculous. Yet, this is what the D.A.R.E. program and the "war on drugs" seems determined to do.

§

Ecstasy: Romeo and I acquired "rolls" at a local summer music festival.[52] Soon after, we created a safe space in our St. Cloud apartment. The Built to Spill album *There's Nothing Wrong with Love* served as our soundtrack. We scattered Legos across our beige carpeted living room floor.

---

52. This was not our first rodeo at this event. The first time we went to the 10,000 Lakes Festival in Detroit Lakes, Minnesota, was in 2004. Were you there? Did you see The Roots perform? If so, we may have shared the same joint.

The white dots slid down our throats, then sailed our bloodstreams. We connected our souls in addition to Lego pieces, crossing the MDMA[53] bridge together. Surrounding the beams, lyrics filled the air, pouring into our bones:

Stay with me until I die. There's nothing else I wanna try.

§

Neuroscience has shown our brains are not fully developed until around the age of 25. This fun fact is the reason I insisted my boyfriend Derek, who I started dating when I was 21, not propose to me until I reached this age. I wanted all my decision-making skills intact before making such a huge life decision.

Perhaps it's no coincidence that by this magical age of 25, drugs had lost most of their appeal. The novelty wore off. I relegated DXM to a time and place with zero interest in carrying its experimentation beyond adolescence. Weed made me too tired and inspired more anxiety than giddiness. Hallucinogens required too much of a time commitment.

I worked at companies with policies outlining their rights to random drug testing. If I wished to indulge in "street" drugs, I would need to drink gallons of water, maybe even buy one of those questionable cleanses from a local pipe store before nervously handing over my cup full of urine and secrets. Doing drugs started to seem less like a leisure activity and more like work.

I still love the release of intoxication and won't deny that using substances to ease banalities, amplify events, and medicate uncomfortable feelings and environments remains sexy to me. I dabble in naughty substances from time to time but now I usually (see below) stick to the boring socially acceptable kinds: alcohol, caffeine, and purified sugar.[54]

---

53. The official chemical name of "Ecstasy."

54. Recently, I've added marijuana edibles to this list because dispensary weed

§

Molly[55]: I am 34 years old and have made the decision to try Molly for the first time. It has been approximately 15 years since my one and only MDMA foray. I need to feel as in control of being out of control as possible. The day before, I weigh out my dose on a gram scale and fill an emptied magnesium capsule with the magical white powder. My friend Annika and boyfriend Daniel[56] plan to split the remaining crystals, simply by eyeing them. Such brave souls!

That night, I text my husband Derek.

11:28pm - Me: I am texting Romeo and he's talking me down from my Molly panic. I just need 100 more people to assure me that I'll be fine. Haha!

Derek: You will be fine. It's just drugs and you over think.

Me: Start a petition!

Derek: K

11:29pm - Me: I know. The worst thing that might happen is a panic attack. I just fear those.

The next text I receive from Derek is a link to a petition on change.org: "Tell Justine Molly is fine" with the subtext, "Justine is concerned about doing a small amount of Molly with friends, it will be fine." The goal number of supporters? One hundred, of course.

11:33pm: No. Please make that go away! I was kidding.

---

gummies are kind of amazing.

55. Molly is the powdered/crystal form of MDMA while Ecstasy comes in pressed pills. Many users assume Molly is "pure" MDMA, but, both Molly and Ecstasy are often cut with other substances.

56. I am polyamorous, by the way. Sorry to spring this on you, reader. How confusing to read about my husband and boyfriend in the same segment. I promise I'll explain myself in the next chapter.

11:35pm: Delete!

Hello?

Please!

11:36pm: My anxiety is growing now

11:39pm: I can't sleep until this is solved

Derek is hanging out with our mutual friend, Brittany. I text her to tell Derek to look at his phone. She assures me it's been taken care of.

I review the Molly subreddit to make sure I have all my bases covered.

Gatorade to maintain electrolytes? Check!

Ginger to help with nausea? Check!

Gum in case of jaw clenching? Dammit. Forgot about that one.

And now for a bedtime story: *The terrified woman was nestled haphazardly in bed while visions of worst-case scenarios danced in her head.*

I turn off my lamp and begin the process of tossing and turning. I have a nightmare in which I take so many drugs I become incapacitated and vomit all over the bathroom. My friends leave me, and I'm forced to embrace the idea I might die. What's done is done.

Final score? Four hours of sleep.

The next evening, Annika, Daniel, and I swallow our pills and venture out on a nature walk. Our friend Mark joins us in spirit with his PBR pounder and joint. Upon our return, we sit down to play a new board game. As I struggle to read the instructions, I realize the drugs must be kicking in.

I stand up and wobble over to a counter, holding on to it, as if it's a mast in a sea storm. I don't mention that I'm freaking out as I stumble over to hug Daniel for several minutes. Suddenly, I feel better. *Way* better. Look up "wellbeing" in the dictionary and you'll see a picture of me on Molly. We float outside to dance to my perfectly curated playlist[57] and gaze at the brilliant orange summer moon illuminating miles of tall prairie grass. I sip orange Gatorade for hydration, which is important, because I cannot stop dancing barefoot on the wooden deck. According to my altered state, touching people is mandatory. I hug my friends and desperately want to climb Daniel like a tree as I wrap my leg around his. How do I entangle our limbs enough to feel as entwined as my body demands? Spoon's Britt Daniel narrates my experience:

I summon you to appear, my Love.

§

In the U.S., D.A.R.E. remains the most prevalent drug education program taught in schools. My dream is that Safety First, or a similar approach, will soon dismantle that trend.

I hope by the time my daughter enters high school (circa 2031), she will have to ask what the letters on my D.A.R.E. ribbon stand for, because the program will be obsolete. She'll laugh when I explain that "back in my day," marijuana was often portrayed as more dangerous than pharmaceutical drugs, even when pharmaceuticals were cited as a leading cause of death two years before her birth. She won't believe it when I tell her these deaths included patients who took the proper dose recommended by their doctors, and I won't blame her.

§

---

57. Including "Take Ecstasy with Me" by The Magnetic Fields because I'm so literal it hurts sometimes.

This piece is not designed to encourage drug use, nor is it meant to serve as a cautionary tale. Chasing the white rabbit is fun, but I'm grateful I've never struggled to climb back out of his lair. I aim to convey this: Drugs don't *always* fuck people up (in the long term).[58] Certain maligned substances, such as marijuana and psilocybin, have proven their ability to reinvigorate an ailing person's quality of life. And sometimes, fucked up people just like to do drugs. Life's a trip, dude. So chill out, and let me enjoy the ride.

---

58. This probably goes without saying, but if drugs didn't fuck you up in the short term, most wouldn't bother with them.

is for Take This Waltz

Reconciling the erotic and the domestic is not a problem that you solve. It is a paradox that you manage.

-Esther Perel, Mating in Captivity

"You should date Derek. I want him to have a nice girlfriend," my friend Megan says.

"I don't think Derek would like me."

I had broken up with my boyfriend Romeo just a few months prior, but the matchmaking efforts were already underway—

Derek and I started dating six months later in January of 2009.

§

Our shared sense of humor became instantly apparent. We planned a "terrible date" in which I dressed like a "slut"[59]

---

59. I'm older and wiser now. If the definition of "slut" is a sexually liberated woman having as much sex as she wants with whoever she wants, sluts are cool AF.

and Derek dressed like a "douchebag." The average American was a caricature to us. The goal of the date was to engage in clichéd dating tropes while mocking consumerism along the way. I wore a short gray skirt, thigh-high tights with tall black boots, and a bright yellow tank top with a plunging neckline. He wore khakis, a brown buttoned-up shirt with the first few buttons undone, and a thin chain necklace.

Derek and I started our date at Bennigans, an Irish pub-inspired restaurant chain, indulging in bacon cheeseburgers and Bananas Foster for dessert. We planned to walk around the mall together but instead smoked too much weed and decided we couldn't handle that kind of environment. As our high simmered, we bought tickets to see the movie *Bride Wars*, a ridiculous film about two women fighting over a specific June wedding date at "the plaza" of their childhood dreams. We shelled out extra dollars to see this masterpiece on a larger screen with louder sound and bought popcorn, even though we were stuffed from supper. After the movie, we drove to a trendy bar we liked to make fun of and then to a dance club full of grinding, horny humans and atrocious music. I had never before embarked on a social experiment in the name of love. This boy understood me.

§

Derek loves metal, and I love indie rock. He relishes parties, and I crave books. We joke our compatibility lies within our mutual hatred for things: silly things like Nickelback and *Live Laugh Love* décor and important things like greedy corporations and political agendas that compromise civil rights.

Derek taught me what a healthy partnership looks like. During the post-Romeo madness, I confided in Derek about struggling to get over Romeo and our toxic past. He listened. I warned him I often get bored in relationships. He stayed.

Derek and I got married in September of 2012.

§

New love remains my favorite drug. Marriage offers a stable love that is more authentic and enduring but also boring to my endorphin-hungry brain. One of my favorite pastimes is consuming art in which the halo of limerence shines bright. Recently, I rewatched *Take This Waltz*, a movie which centers around a married woman named Margot (Michelle Williams) falling for an artist (Luke Kirby) who lives across the street.

§

When Derek and I first started dating, he discussed the future possibility of having a threesome or engaging in a couple's sex swap.

"I don't want to watch you have sex with anyone else and I think it's weird you'd want to watch me have sex with someone else," I replied, defensive.

I also made it clear I was not comfortable with him going to strip clubs because it was a cultural loophole that favored men. For most women (I assume?), male strippers are a source of comedic entertainment, not arousal. I insisted I should be allowed to grind against random men at the bar if going to a strip club was considered okay. Derek understood my point and respected it. No lap dances for him.

Fast forward to our 7th wedding anniversary. The 7-year itch: alive and well. We went to a strip club together. I had never been to one before and wanted to see what all the fuss was about. No alcohol was allowed inside, so I took shots of vodka in the parking lot before entering. I was the only woman voyeur, which was a bit unsettling. The experience was mildly entertaining, lackluster. Derek didn't want a lap dance and neither did I. It seemed like a waste of money.

§

Derek and I had grown apart, the sexual chemistry lost somewhere between child rearing and staring at screens in lieu of speaking to each other. Derek spent his days working long hours at the office. I stayed home with our daughter Ivy, bored out of my skull, playing Cinderella and Candy Land. When Ivy was an infant, Derek and I tag teamed bedtime. Eventually, desperate for quality "me" time, we decided to alternate days. When Derek put Ivy to bed, I escaped to the movie theater or attended writer's group meetings. On Derek's nights off, he biked to his favorite brewery or carved wood into oars in his friend's garage. It was the perfect plan! Except for the part where we rarely spent time *together*. And when we did, the pressure to prove we were still a couple centered around our sex life.

Derek purchased expensive sex toys for us to try, hopeful the "dirty thirties" would transform me into a sex goddess. Meanwhile, I was certain sex was overrated and dull and who the hell has time for such nonsense?

I'm not sure when our marital dissatisfaction became too blaring to ignore, but once the concept was introduced, it opened the floodgates for potential solutions. When I call the EAP to schedule our first counseling session, they ask what the issue is.

"I'm not really sure. Communication, maybe?"

Our couple's counselor suggests we kiss mindfully for two minutes a day. Every female friend I tell this to scrunches their nose up in reply. Good, I'm not the only one who hates this idea.

"Nudes?" Derek requests via text, while on a break at work.

Sigh.

§

Early in our courtship, Derek introduced me to *Café Flesh*, an '80s sci-fi cult porno that centers around two groups of humans: Sex Positives and Sex Negatives. Sex Negatives can look, but they cannot touch, and they succumb to a violent illness if they have sex. As a result, the Sex Positives put on elaborate sex theatre for their viewing pleasure. Suffice to say, I'm a Sex Negative married to a Sex Positive.

Do I ever enjoy sex? Sure, if certain conditions are met. The relationship must be relatively new and/or:

1. There must be substances involved.
2. There must be a killer playlist in the background.
3. I need to have showered and shaved recently.
4. It needs to be dim in the room so you can barely see me.
5. I need to be within my fertile window.
6. I can't be too stressed or tired or bloated or in pain.
7. My daughter can't be awake or expected to wake up soon.
8. I can't already be touched out for the day (a common reality for the introverted mother of a young, needy child).
9. I can't be annoyed about the laundry you left piled on the bed again. *Just leave the clothes in the basket if you aren't going to fold them and put them away!*
10. Hayley's comet needs to be visible from Earth. (I *suppose* I can be flexible on this one.)

Otherwise, I lie there thinking about the dishes I should finish or the dental appointment I need to make for my daughter in the morning or how much easier masturbation is. Can't we just watch a movie and cuddle on the couch instead?

§

"Let's watch this TED talk," Derek says, pulling up *Monogamish: The New Rules of Marriage* on my laptop. The speaker (Jessica O'Reilly, sexologist) introduces us to "monogamish": a partnership that is generally monogamous, but which may have rare sexual interactions outside of the relationship. The term monogamish was coined by sex writer Dan Savage.

According to Mr. Savage, until the twentieth century, most cultures granted men the ability to be non-monogamous without consequence. Males couldn't help it. It was part of their inherent nature! However, women were expected to remain monogamous to guarantee paternity, controlling their sexuality.

Cheating is a common phenomenon among long-term "monogamous" couples, but the component of infidelity that causes the most damage is the breach of trust, not the sex itself. And so, a radical concept is introduced: what if each couple designed their own relationship, standard definitions be damned? Enter: ethical non-monogamy.

Derek and I watch a monogamish documentary together. We devour the fictional Netflix series *Easy*, featuring a married couple who decide to try an open relationship. *Easy* depicts the pros and cons of various relationship styles in a non-contrived manner. I skim *The Ethical Slut*, a polyamory[60] guide.

I insist we need ground rules if this is going to work. I've been cheated on in the past (by someone else), and while I trust Derek, I'm insecure and tend to let my imagination run

---

60. Polyamory is the practice of having multiple sexual and/or loving relationships at the same time with the knowledge and consent of all involved.

wild with what ifs. We sit down with our booze (beer for Derek, vodka for me) and a couple index cards. The rules start out PG. We can make out with people and flirt with the same person on an ongoing basis. But eventually, we grow bolder.

§

In high school, I wore hemp necklaces religiously. I assumed my midlife crisis might involve a return to this trend, a nostalgic throwback to my young hippie self. Instead, it involved sending nudes to an ex from high school who *still* wears them.

I dated Vaughan for a whole week my sophomore year before deciding I wasn't ready to be someone's girlfriend. Around the time Derek and I opened our marriage, Vaughan and I reconnected on Facebook. He regaled us with tales of his polyamorous lifestyle, something he adopted after his divorce. It soon became clear Vaughan wanted a sexual relationship with me. I liked being wanted, but flirting was all I could commit to since I wasn't attracted to him. Hence, the nudes.

Derek beat me to anything physical, making out and getting handsy with a mutual friend who initiated things. I thought I was going to be the first person to get kissed, but it seems I was too picky/insecure/myself to make it happen.

§

In *Take This Waltz*, when Margot's husband discovers she has been pining after another man, he tells her to go to him. He wants her to be happy.

§

Shortly before Derek and I opened our marriage, I developed a crush on my friend Daniel. I tried to ignore this budding desire for about a year-and-a-half before gaining the courage to do anything about it. I figured he represented a mirage in the desert, forbidden fruit on the tree of life. If I just kissed him, I could *get over it already!* Instead, when I finally gained the resolve to kiss him (after weeks of flirting and an evening in which I consumed four alcoholic beverages), I discovered I was in love with him. Whoops!

I hoped the infatuation would fade. In the meantime, I distanced myself from Derek. How could I break this news to him? He knew I had a crush on Daniel and had kissed him, but he didn't know the extent of my feelings. After a week of internal struggle (and some frazzled text messages to my best friend), I told Derek we needed to talk.

"You're not divorcing me, are you?" Derek asks.

"No, it's not that."

"You're in love with Daniel?"

"Uh. Yeeeaahh?—"

"Oh, that's fine!" Derek said with a sigh of relief.

"Is it?!"

"Yeah, it makes sense."

With Derek's blessing, I started dating Daniel and our monogamish relationship quickly spiraled into a polyamorous one.

§

If I left my husband for a passionate romance with the artist across the street (or in my case, the radio DJ from across town), would the ending disappoint me? Infatuation is a temporary state of insanity, and like Margot, I too am *restless in a kind of permanent way.* Now that Pandora's box has been opened, monogamy feels a bit like an itchy sweater I've outgrown, and I fear a return to it would lead to claustrophobia.

After the sparkle of Margot's new relationship fades, she returns to her husband, asking if he'd consider taking her back. He denies her.

Margot's sister-in-law, Geraldine, sees Margot standing outside the house. Geraldine pulls her aside, offering these words of wisdom:

"You think that everything can be worked out if you just make the right move?...Life has a gap in it. It just does. You don't go crazy trying to fill it like some lunatic."

Well said, Geraldine. Well said.

But what if you can build a bridge over that gap, respecting its existence while innovating a structure to reimagine it?

This to me, is polyamory.

Derek wanted more sex and I wanted to give him that—just not with me, all the time. I wanted novel romantic experiences—just not with him, all the time.

§

I love my husband and I love my boyfriend. These are not mutually exclusive statements. How do I know this? Because I live this truth. If you have two children, do you love one more than the other? Is one *better* than the other? Nope, they're just different. Meaningful relationships are not created via cookie cutters. Love is not a finite resource.

Derek gives me full-body massages to help keep my chronic pain at bay. He fixes cars for friends and strangers who can't afford it, donates produce from our (honestly, his) garden, and enjoys planting trees to help save the planet in his spare time. He helped me bring a hilarious, strong-willed, smart, cute little human into the world. We both love stand-up comedy. I can tell him anything.

Daniel is an avid reader who also enjoys writing. He introduces me to films and music that make me excited to be alive. He understands I'm a delicate fucking flower and does his best to accommodate me. He takes me on fun, lovely dates and sings "Love Shack" with me at karaoke. He inspired me to ditch Spotify and Amazon and buy more music and books from local establishments and/or directly from the artists themselves.

Both Derek and Daniel crack me up, shower me with compliments, and care about the environment as much as I do. They are giving lovers who are supportive of my creative endeavors. Society says I must choose between these two men I love. Why? Because monogamy is the only script we have read.

§

In her book *What Love is and What it Could Be*, philosopher Carrie Jenkins draws parallels between the stigma associated with polyamory and same-sex attraction. During the 2015 federal debate over the issue of same sex marriage, gay people who identified as polyamorous found it necessary to distance themselves from that part of their identity, promoting instead "a narrative of queer love that very closely resembles 'traditional' monogamous romance." Any connection between gay marriage and polyamory may have sullied the legal progress being made in the queer community.

The monogamy narrative of romantic love is too ingrained in our collective consciousness to make room for people who dare to love more than one person of the same gender *gasp* *at the same time.* But some polyamorous people claim they are wired that way, that it's an integral part of their sexual orientation. Derek and I made a conscious decision to embrace this type of lifestyle, but for some, it's the only way they know how to love.

§

Admittedly, polyamory is not for everyone, especially the faint of heart. There's nothing wrong with monogamy for those who wish to practice it. But what about the rest of us?

According to a 2021 study, polyamory is gaining ground in the United States. Approximately 11% of Americans have been in a polyamorous relationship and about 17% would like to try one.

§

Isn't it hard to share someone you love with someone else?

You betcha! It's hard to shake off a monogamy hangover. We've suffered growing pains, especially because Derek and I stumbled upon a fully open relationship unexpectedly and some of our ("progressive") family and friends have not been supportive. I've endured the sensation of an invisible scarlet "A" being stapled to my chest.

What about the children?! (Or in my case, the child)

Everyone approaches polyamory in their own way. Some partners choose to live together with their kids, creating one large family unit. Others prefer more separation and discretion. We fit into the latter category. My husband and I both like to go out with friends on a regular basis. As far as our 5-year-old kiddo is concerned, Derek and I just have a lot of "friends." The specifics of what we do with our friends behind closed doors isn't anybody's business but our own.

As our daughter gets older, she may catch on to our unconventional lifestyle, but we won't worry about navigating that terrain until we stumble upon it.

Don't I get jealous?

Of course, I do.

Derek recently started building a relationship with a fellow plant-lover who co-owns an art gallery/brewery in Canada. They share a love of history, beer, and homesteading. She's an artist and a writer, with a fascinating blog that chronicles her unorthodox upbringing. I can't compete with her. But as Derek is always reminding me, it's *not* a competition.

§

A few weeks after Derek becomes infatuated with "the Canadian", a panic attack jolts me awake in the middle of the night. I creep over to Derek's side of the bed and snatch his phone from the bedside table. I *must* see what he's been saying to her.

"What are you doing?" Derek asks, bleary-eyed and barely conscious.

"I need to read your messages from [the Canadian]."

"It's going to be hard to see. There's been some flirting," Derek says.

"I don't care. I *have* to read them."

This is an agreement we made ahead of time. We are allowed to read each other's text messages[61] to prove we aren't hiding anything, such as secret plans to move to another country to be with another lover (for example). I didn't find any evidence of this in the conversation I read and the Canadian was aware of our texting rules, so I wasn't doing anything *wrong* per say. But I still felt pathetic and guilty for prying into their relationship.

§

Jealousy is not a warm, comfortable feeling, so I understand why people are reluctant to embrace it, but are monogamous relationships void of this feeling? Daniel identifies as mo-

---

61. With some exceptions

nogamous, but my stomach still rises to my throat at the sight of women he's crushed on. My heart races at the mention of women he's been with. I compare my pale blemished skin to the flawless olive complexion of Ana de Armas (his "celebrity girlfriend").

Is discomfort not a side effect of personal growth?

When I sit with my jealousy and tease it apart with a fine-toothed comb, it gives way to enlightened revelations. *Why* am I jealous? Because I struggle with low self-esteem? I live in a misogynistic culture that encourages women to compete against one another for male attention? I have an insecure attachment style that demands your undivided attention and makes me want to run away at the slightest hint of rejection? Check. Check. Check.!!

Polyamory gives me the gift of owning my body, bestows upon me the reward of allowing my lovers to receive more love than I can give.

It takes strong limbs and coordination to withstand the weight of a polyamorous lifestyle. And while audience members occasionally throw tomatoes at us, causing us to lose our balance and step on each other's feet, I couldn't ask for two better dance partners.

May I have this dance?

U

is for Umbilical Cord

The birth of my daughter Ivy traumatized me. I hoped for a more granola experience, as promised by the *Business of Being Born* DVD. But the bullet points on my birth plan contracted alongside my uterus. I still wonder how I would have weathered the storm of new life under better circumstances: a good night's sleep beforehand, a baby in the proper position. Instead, Ivy had to be cut out of my body after 48+ hours of labor. Lamaze classes and prenatal yoga be damned! My body failed to progress, and my psyche rested on eggshells.

§

My husband Derek applied at Microsoft 115 times, and during March of 2016, he received a job offer. Persistence paid off! Either that or the 115th time is the charm. This meant working for a company he respected, that takes good care of its employees. This meant better health insurance with a generous health savings account. This meant when we had a baby, he would get *paid* paternity leave and I could spend more time with my family, instead of working nights and weekends.

Before Derek delivered this news, I came home from a rough day at work, craving oblivion. I entertained the idea of inviting my friend Ryan to meet me at a bar for some vodka shots. But first, I needed to take a pregnancy test. Derek and I had made the decision to stop using birth control a few months before, and my period was overdue. I figured the odds of pregnancy were slim, but it seemed necessary to rule it out before poisoning myself on purpose.

After Derek told me about his upcoming career shift, we were ecstatic. Still buzzing from the announcement, I joked:

"Now I'm going to take this pregnancy test, and it's going to be positive!" *Hahahahaha!*

...

Well, what do you know?

As Derek likes to say, within 24 hours, "we went from zero to adult." All at once, everything in our universe aligned.

No vodka shots for me. I made plans to play pinochle with my friend Amber instead and spilled the beans immediately. She insisted we name the baby "Bernie" to honor the presidential candidate we all loved, the one (~~who got away~~) later forced out during the primaries.

§

During my pregnancy, I kept a cool head. Disregard moments of frazzled panic when my baby didn't kick often enough. Dismiss all the Google searches about babies who never engage in the pelvis (*Umbilical cord prolapse?! Pre-emptive scheduled C-section?!*). Never mind all the gnawing reminders that even after a healthy first trimester, there are no guarantees. I tried my best to remain distant from the creature growing inside me, but I wanted and loved this baby too much already. At night, I stroked my belly while lying in bed. *Are you an Ivy or a Ryker?*

§

On a Wednesday morning, four days after my official due date, I stared at my phone in defeat while lying on my bed. The results of the 2016 presidential election stared back, taunting me beyond my bulging belly. *Ugh.* My body discomfort gained a new rival: my brain discomfort after processing those results. It meant my daughter *would* be born into a country which had given up on that whole "justice for all" jazz. It meant my daughter *could* have been born into a country where climate change was appreciated as the behemoth crisis it is, but instead would be dismissed by our new leader as a "hoax." It meant that once again, American progress leapt one step forward only to be promptly shoved two steps back.

Texts streamed in from friends and family. Many of them stated the same thing: "I cried when I saw the results." On that Wednesday night, my labor pains began in earnest. I received little sleep as they raged. Soon, my little "Bernie" would be forced out too.

On Thursday, I continued having contractions. Mild during the day, they started to pick up in intensity toward nightfall. Around midnight, I suspected my water broke. *Yikes!*

Derek drove me to the hospital, but it turned out to be a false alarm. My water bag remained intact, and my nurse discovered I was only 1.5 centimeters dilated.[62] We accepted the option of pacing the maternity ward for an hour to see if I would make any progress, but walking failed to expedite my labor, so they sent us home.

That night, there would be zero sleep. My fierce contractions would not allow it. I spent an hour sitting on the floor of my shower, letting hot water cascade over my protruding belly until it ran cool. Emily, my gray-and-white cat, served as

---

62. You must be at 10 to push out a baby.

my doula. She followed me around the house, looking concerned while I wailed out at random intervals.

The next morning, Derek brought me to the OB clinic for a scheduled appointment. I started crying, feeling hysterical in front of my midwife. I explained I'd hardly slept in 2 days. She insisted on checking my cervix, though I doubted any overnight progress.

"You're at 3 centimeters, so I'm admitting you. We can break your water to speed up your contractions and order an epidural, so you can get some rest."

We checked into our labor room around 10:30 in the morning. I let them break my water bag but declined the epidural. My mother survived natural childbirth with all three of her daughters, and I hoped to tap into my genetic potential to do the same.

The whirlpool bath served as my haven. I refused solid food but sipped on orange Gatorade. My contractions became more manageable when surrounded by hot water, jet streams, and relaxing white noise. My left arm, sporting my IV hep lock, draped over the side of the tub. Previous IV placement attempts resulted in large purple bruises, spidering out from the crook of my right arm.

As a child, I feared childbirth because of the necessity of an IV. Ha! An IV is like a pinprick compared to the hell of uterine contractions. Of course, a prepubescent child is clueless about these things.

After laboring another four or five hours, I researched the pros and cons of epidurals on my smartphone.

Some women warriors use "magical" to describe their childbirth experience, but I would never use that word to describe what happened within my body. My innards resembled a battleground from which there was no escape. I asked my labor nurse to summon the anesthesiologist.

Within minutes of having the epidural placed, my pain melted away. I regained hope, and an appetite. They placed me on a clear liquid diet, and I eagerly awaited the arrival of my dinner tray while watching *The Simpsons*. My food arrived around 7:30pm. I noshed away on cherry gelatin and chicken broth. Then, I attempted to "rest" (see: impossible).

My midwife checked my progress.

"You're still at 3.5 cm," she said, sympathetic.

I was started on 2 units of Pitocin, a drug often used to induce or accelerate labor.

After my due date came and went at 40 weeks, I dreaded the possibility of induction. Remaining pregnant up to 41 weeks in a low-risk pregnancy is considered safe, but the research becomes murky between 41 and 42 weeks. I had scoured the Internet for info, attempting to weigh the pros and cons of induction versus waiting for nature to take its course. I never arrived at an answer.

I wished to avoid Pitocin, which inspires stronger contractions and forces them closer together. These effects translated into an increased potential for fetal distress. But I was so very tired of being in labor, so here we were.

Things improved when I dilated to 6 cm within an hour. But then, my labor stalled again, so they bumped the Pitocin dose up to 4 units.

Intermittently, a few nurses would tag team the task of moving me from laying on one side to my other side.

Suddenly, a phone removed from its cradle: hushed, urgent voices summoning more staff into the room. My baby's heartbeat dipping, each slow beat punctuating my panic.

The meaning of helpless redefined. The lower half of my body paralyzed, breathing desperately into an oxygen mask as I pleaded with the universe. *No. No. No. Please. Please. Please.*

"Let's get you on your hands and knees!" a nurse said, trying to sound reassuring, though it seemed she meant to reassure herself as well.

The nurses arranged my body into a hands-and-knees position. After an eternity, my daughter's heartbeat normalized. Perhaps it took only a few minutes, but time is relative. The Pitocin had to be stopped since it stressed my little peanut out. So once again, labor stalled.

I started to experience horrendous back labor, the worst physical pain I've known. I groaned, I cried, I dug my nails into Derek's skin and gripped the bed railing as if grounding myself during a passing tornado. The only thing that made the pain bearable was a heating pad and strong counter pressure applied to my back by an OB nurse, an angel named Beth. Her technique was fantastic. Whenever anyone else stepped in, I wanted to scream. Although Derek got the hang of it eventually.

My baby was sunny side-up, and the epidural could not erase the searing pain that went along with her malpositioned body. One repetitive thought: *Just cut her out of me!*

The back labor caused me to vomit profusely, all the liquids slurped down a couple hours prior, gone within a few minutes of heaving.

My progress halted. 9 cm. Stuck.

"You're almost there. Just a little bit longer," my midwife and nurses offered.

I never questioned their confidence. But *How?! How would*

I push a baby out? My back pain and sleep deprivation disabled me. Miracle of childbirth indeed.

The back labor intensified. 9cm. Trapped.

My midwife asked the question I waited for:

"Do you want me to call in the surgeon?"

When you fantasize about the type of birth you'd like to have, few people aim for invasive abdominal surgery. But it's all relative.

"How long does a C-section take?" I gasped, hoping this hell might end.

"About 45 minutes."

Fucking. Sign. Me. Up!

More paperwork. Blah blah blah…serious risks…blah blah blah…

Being carted through the halls gave me *ER* flashbacks. Sadly, there was no George Clooney or Noah Wyle in sight. The nurses wheeled me into a freezing room where I received spinal anesthesia. It spread all the way to my fingers, numbing them along with my floating limbs.

"I feel like I can't breathe," I said.

"That's just the anesthesia making it hard to feel yourself breathing. Your oxygen levels are fine. We're watching them."

I believed her but found it hard to focus on anything else. Perceived suffocation can have that effect.

Ivy Linn was born at 4:37am, on a Saturday morning at 41 weeks gestation. She cried, and my heart soared. She passed meconium in the womb, so her nose and throat needed to be suctioned out. Because of the urgency of the situation, delayed cord clamping was not in the cards. Birth plan idea # infinity out the window.

The nurses placed Ivy across my chest for some skin-to-skin. A wiry little thing at 6 lbs, 1 oz, she was pale with huge blue eyes that pierced into my soul when I met her gaze.

"Oh my God, I LOVE HER!"

Some women fall instantly in love with their babies while others form a gradual bond. I had given myself permission not to feel guilty either way. But here we were. My love for this little person registered without effort. My heart ached with growing pains while my anxiety roared into overdrive.

§

In a follow-up visit to my room, my midwife explained how my surgery revealed my uterus to be positioned in a "weird place." I imagined car anatomy: engines tucked away in inconvenient spaces under the hood. *Who the hell decided to put that there?* No wonder Ivy never fully engaged in my pelvis, and the contractions grew stronger to no avail. My midwife advised I opt for scheduled C-sections in the future to avoid any repeats of that labor shit show[63].

I had heard about the baby blues but hadn't expected to teeter on the verge of a nervous breakdown. During the entire hospital stay, sleep remained elusive. Bright lights streamed from the charting computer and call light system, shining in the direction of my bed. Through the walls, I heard the muffled sounds of crying babies and heartbeat monitors. A constant parade of staff filed through my room to check vitals, draw blood, and administer gruesome uterine massages. Finding a comfortable position was impossible while tethered to multiple devices. An IV in my arm, an oxygen mon-

---

63. I'm paraphrasing.

itor clipped to my toe, compression pants which made me sweat, and a urinary catheter. I slept approximately 3 hours over the 4 days I was hospitalized, growing more insane by the minute.

Discussing the details of the birth tore my chest open. When Ivy cried, I sobbed, feeling helpless. One night during our hospital stay, Derek brought Ivy to the nurse's station to give me a chance to sleep. Instead, I bawled uncontrollably.

I was famished but not allowed to eat a proper meal until I "passed gas." Before my bowels were in working order, I lived on blueberry and cherry Chobani yogurt cups and cranberry juice. I developed a nostalgic fondness for these items: tying them to my daughter like others link a fudge recipe to their grandmother.

One of the lactation consultants kneaded my breasts so hard, my guts wrenched. Three days after Ivy was born, we discovered she was starving. I hadn't produced enough colostrum to meet her needs, so we had to supplement with donor breast milk and formula until my milk came in. This made me feel like a failure as a woman. I couldn't birth my own baby nor meet her needs. I understood I was being hard on myself, but the hysteria created by my hormones and insomnia prevailed.

I tried reassuring myself by focusing on the promised comforts of home. I grieved over my loss of control, all the disappointments between my birthing expectations and the harsh reality I endured. Derek and the nursing staff helped me cope. Their amazing support prevented my fraying self from unraveling completely.

I still remember many of the names and faces of the nurses who took care of me:

    1. Kayla - She convinced me there was no shame in choosing formula over breastfeed-

ing, allowing me to have compassion for my-self.

2. Kaylee - She worked in the NICU and se-cured donor breast milk for Ivy. Her personal life reminded me of a lovely, albeit cliché, love story. Her husband served in the mili-tary, and she was a bubbly nurse on a mater-nity ward, with a radiant glow and an ador-able baby bump in tow.

3. Beth – See above about her role in my back labor and look up "saint" in the dictionary.

4. Abby - She had a good sense of humor and ran us through our discharge paperwork.

If I had the means, I would have bought these women all-expense-paid vacations or, at the very least, Target gift cards. Instead, Derek and I bought a heartfelt thank-you card to send them, but it got lost in the shuffle of new parenthood and never made its way to the post office. The best we could offer was the complimentary mini cake the food service staff delivered to our room and our eternal gratitude.

The day before my scheduled discharge date, my blood pres-sure read high for the first time since becoming pregnant: physical evidence of my severe stress and insomnia. I wor-ried they weren't going to let me leave, although I seemed more worked up about it than the nursing staff. The next day, Derek and I were sent home to care for our little human all by ourselves.

§

While taking my first shower upon arriving home, Ivy's cry looped through my brain. How would I sustain another hu-man while failing to keep myself afloat? I took an hour-long nap and awoke with an overwhelming sense of dread. Would

I ever feel "normal" again? I fretted over the possibility of further hospitalization due to potential postpartum complications.

My nerves burned raw, and my appetite disappeared. Not having any food in my system made the uneasiness worse, my blood sugar a nightmare. My mother-in-law dropped off a sausage white bean soup, and it was one of the only things I could stand. While eating, I found it necessary to immerse myself in sorting papers, to distract my attention from the unrelenting nausea.

I didn't eat enough calories and struggled to take a daily multivitamin to replenish my nutrient stores. The lactation consultant gave me a pumping goal of eight times per day *in addition* to regular breastfeeding sessions to promote milk production.[64] On a good day, I maxed out at three.

Ivy cluster-fed, a horrible phenomenon in which a baby insists on being attached to your boob for *several* hours at a time. I wanted to stab my eyes out and fantasized about letting go of my desire to exclusively breastfeed and use formula instead.

I studied the ingredients in Ivy's formula, frowning.

"Derek, we give higher-quality food to our cat."[65]

Cloth diapers were not going to happen as planned. Charting Ivy's disposable diapers didn't happen either nor did we change her enough. We didn't know when she wet her diapers, failing to notice the indicator strips designed for that purpose. We didn't feed her every two hours as advised. We stopped giving her feedings via syringe and switched to bot-

---

64. Breastfeeding is traditionally advertised as an effortless, natural process. For many women, it is *not*.

65. I don't mean to sound like a sanctimommy. There's nothing wrong with using formula. It's just not what I wanted.

tles, succumbing to the dangers of nipple confusion.[66] I had been a parent for less than a week and felt I was already failing at it. It was. All. Too. Much.

When Ivy was 2 weeks old, I stayed home with her while Derek went to a Henry Rollins[67] talk. Alone with my baby for the first time, I aimed to ignore the terror of my parental incompetence. I fended off a full-blown panic attack by watching *Parks and Recreation* and talking to my cousin Becca on the phone. I distinctly remember our conversation including my newfound, sage advice: "Don't have kids."

Ivy suffered from reflux. At night, she made grunting noises in her co-sleeper beside me. Occasionally, she coughed and sounded as if she might choke on regurgitated milk. My breathing seized at the sound. Derek snored while I breastfed. I tried to hold Ivy upright for at least 20 minutes after every feeding. I relied on the 4am company provided by mom chat forums. I swore to never co-sleep. I swore to wean her when she turned one. But ultimately, I did whatever it took to survive, which meant co-sleeping and breastfeeding on demand, and of course, lots of actual swearing.[68]

§

Ivy is now a preschooler. When she was a toddler, I still struggled to shed my worries. I had the luxury of staying home with her during the week and only allowed her grandparents to babysit for short periods. Nobody put Ivy to bed other than her father and/or me for the first couple years of her life.

---

66. Look it up. It's a thing.

67. A man of many talents, Henry Rollins is a spoken word artist, musician, actor, writer, television and radio host, and comedian.

68. Women and their partners are encouraged to monitor for symptoms of postpartum depression. However, I never heard the term post-partum anxiety, which I *clearly* suffered from, until after I went through it myself.

Derek insisted we needed more time away from her. He wanted to catch an evening movie and plan weekend getaways. I insisted our baby would only be a baby for a short time, and I wasn't ready. To relinquish my illusion of control over her wellbeing filled me with a restless apprehension. I wanted Ivy to be able to verbalize her own feelings before handing the reins over. I couldn't stand the idea of her being hurt or scared, her needs misunderstood. I craved an excessive amount of reassurance as a child and couldn't stomach the idea of Ivy crying herself to sleep, yearning for me: her preferred safety blanket.

A difficult birth and my subsequent reactions to parenting have scarred my body and my mind. I have decided not to have any more children, partially because there is no guarantee my sanity would survive another round. I love my husband and daughter, and I'm not willing to take that chance.

Since Ivy's birth, this cord of hypervigilance connecting me to my daughter has lost some of its strength. With Ivy's budding independence, the threads have relaxed. Of course, I'll never sever them completely.

But I wouldn't have it any other way.

$\mathcal{V}$

is for Vacation, Interrupted

In 1993, to celebrate my sixth birthday, my family planned a trip to Orlando Studios in Florida: the perfect destination for a Nickelodeon junkie. With a smile on my face, I left behind the forced naps of kindergarten class and the frigid Minnesota January temperatures.

My mom packed my outfits, preparing for any weather we might encounter. It's the kind of thing mothers, especially those from the Midwest, seem to excel in. Black pants and a light pink jacket? Check. Yellow shorts and a Looney Tunes t-shirt? Check. Hand-me-down green bathing suit with black skirt bottom for the hotel pool? Check. I packed the important stuff: toys I couldn't live without and a few dollars of allowance saved up for souvenirs.

My paternal grandparents joined my parents, older sister Louisa, and me on our adventures. The Griswold vacation type, my family shunned the friendly skies for the cramped quarters of our grandparents' van. We left in the afternoon, driving from my grandparent's house in Clara City, Minnesota to Madison, Wisconsin. Pretty skylines and icy waters.

Southbound through Illinois to Paducah, Kentucky. Rising temps and hills.

I don't remember how my sister and I entertained ourselves on this car ride, but I can wage a guess based on other trips from my childhood. We may have played car games, possibly roping the adults into a few rounds.

"I'm going on a picnic and I'm bringing an apple," I would start.

"I'm going on a picnic and I'm bringing an apple and a blanket," Louisa would reply.

"I'm going on a picnic and I'm bringing an apple, a blanket, and a cat!" my dad would chime in.

I imagine we snacked on frosted strawberry Poptarts straight from the package while setting up a blanket fort that served as a Barbie palace. We spent plenty of time taking naps and staring out the window, marveling at the changing temperatures and terrain as the miles accumulated.

We made it to Nashville by the next morning. Sunshine-streaked mountain views. Southeast to Chattanooga, then on to Atlanta. Gas station attendants who sound funny when they talk. "Ya'll come back now, ya hear?" From Atlanta to Macon. Finally reaching Kissimmee, Florida that evening.

We spent two days exploring Orlando Studios. As we entered the park on the first day, we were greeted by a spinning silver globe with "Orlando Studios" spelled out in gold letters. Louisa and I wore matching outfits: white t-shirts with a paint splatter design and black pants. A black scrunchie secured my poofy blond mane in a ponytail, a thick purple headband guarded my sister's eyes from her wild blond curls.[69] We giggled when Harry from *Harry and the Hendersons* gave

---

69. It's okay to be jealous. '90s fashion was something to behold.

us a smothering hug in front of the *I Love Lucy* museum. Stars bearing celebrity names decorated the ground beneath our feet. Here's Woody Woodpecker! There's Bette Midler.

Louisa and I made silly faces behind wooden character cut-outs at Fievel's playland, a playground inspired by the animated film *Fievel Goes West*.

We caught a live show: Beetlejuice's Rock-and-Roll Graveyard Revue, featuring choreographed dances performed by Frankenstein, his bride, and other ghastly creatures.[70] Those monsters could bust a move![71]

On the second day, my grandparents stayed behind at the hotel.

The rest of us checked out Nickelodeon Studios. Louisa and I got a kick out of the restrooms sign featuring *Ren & Stimpy*. We watched the famous Gak Geyser with fascination, its bright green slime cascading over the odd shaped contraption. Louisa pretended to grab the orange cement flag fastened to the Double Dare obstacle, singing along to the *Clarissa Explains It All* theme song playing over the loud outdoor speaker:

"Nah nah na na nah…nu nu na na na na!"

I purchased a neon green wallet with my precious souvenir money, proudly displaying it in front of my dad's giant video camera.

We participated in a mock version of the Nickelodeon game show: *What Would You Do?* If only given the opportunity to throw a whipped cream pie in someone's face, our experience would have been complete!

---

70. Fun Fact: Years later, Louisa and I would discover that the person behind the werewolf costume was Joey Fatone! He worked that gig at Orlando Studios before joining N'Sync.

71. After re-watching our family vacation video, I also realized Wayne Brady was Dracula!

The first Orlando ride to catch our eye was the *Back to the Future* motion simulator. My mom insisted my dad and Louisa go on the ride without me. She predicted I would not do well on it. Even then, I exhibited an intolerance to overstimulating situations. But my dad trusted my abilities, and according to the height line, I made the cut (by a hair). I studied the large Delorean we would be buckled into. It didn't look *so* scary. There would be no stomach dropping dips or spinning upside down. Best of all, it wasn't enclosed like the Gravitron fair ride I'm still not brave enough to go on.

After getting strapped in and watching the "time machine" doors close around me, I started to question my decision. Directly in front of us, a garage door lifted to reveal a large Imax screen. The lights dimmed to total darkness, and the car began jerking in unison with the film. The images warped my reality, and I soon got lost in the experience. Toward the end of the ride, an angry T-rex catches our flying car in its mouth.

"AHHHHHH," I wailed, confident a dinosaur swallowed us whole.

The ride ended, and the lights flickered on. I lurched around, struggling to make sense of my surroundings as my family tried to calm me. What just happened? How did I get here? The room seemed familiar, with no hungry dinosaur in sight. My panic dissipated with my recovered memory: *Oh yeah. Make-believe.*

After this incident, my parents became wary about which ride to try next. We settled on E.T. Adventure, where you coast through the sky on a bike while your alien friend hangs out in the front basket.

Nobody likes a buzzkill. As we moved along in the line, waiting for our turn to board, I tried to hide my apprehension. I held my mom's hand, no doubt giving myself away through my clammy palms. My heart pulsated in my ears as

I anticipated the scary surprises of unchartered territory. The butterflies in my stomach multiplied as we approached the front. Kids on TV and in real life seemed to get such a kick out of rides. What made me different? What was wrong with *me*?

I climbed onto the "bike," taking a seat beside my mom. We took off with a shaky start, matching the tremble in my body. The exciting surroundings could not compete with my fear. I managed to maintain my composure for a brief time, but there's never a Cat's game scenario when challenging panic. It always wins.

The headlights of a jeep popped up, abrupt and overwhelming my pre-tuned nerves. Suddenly, the bad men who wished to steal E.T. chased after us. Shouting voices and harsh lights accosted me, with no escape in sight. Make-believe or not, I remained trapped, along for the whole ride whether I liked it or not.

"WAAAAHH!" tears sprung from my eyes as my alarm peaked.

My mom tried to comfort me as best she could among the loud noises and shifting movements. I hid by her feet, where the horrors of the ride couldn't reach my eyes. In this (questionably?) safe crevice, I started to relax.

After a few minutes, the signature E.T. theme song began playing, and I reemerged, delighted with the lightened mood. We soared over a beautiful city, which glistened under the glow of a radiant false moon. *Now this is awesome!*

When the ride ended, I squirmed out of my seat and onto the platform, feeling safer on the steady, solid ground.

I didn't go on any more rides that day.

§

My family teases me for harboring a "vacation curse." Evidence:

1. A year or two after the Orlando Studios trip, I battle a stomach bug as my dad carries me around the Minnesota State Fair.

2. In 1998, I sustain severe sun burns during a Myrtle Beach camping trip.

3. In 2001, two weeks after exploring New York City with my dad, older sister, and her friend, the twin towers fall. (See picture above. Eerie, no?)

4. In 2004, after arriving in O'ahu for my cousin's wedding, my neck glands swell up like golf balls and my throat burns raw. Diagnosis? Mononucleosis, the "kissing disease."

5. A few months later, my boyfriend cheats on me as I tour a Disney theme park.

6. In 2007, my heat stroke derails a family trip to Pensacola, Florida.

7. In 2009, my future husband Derek and I camp with friends, and it rains the entire time. Our tent leaks and we sleep in a puddle. Derek and I arrive home feeling like hell. Diagnosis? Swine flu.

8. In 2010, Derek nurses me through a dehydration-inspired panic attack while visiting Glacier National Park. Diagnosis: altitude sickness?

In 2013, I fly to Denver with my mom, sisters, and my mom's best friend. We have a great time, and determine the curse is broken!

§

In January of 2020, my mom and I plan a spring trip to Pensacola, Florida, to visit my Aunt Lori. My 3-year-old daughter Ivy will embark on her first plane trip! My mom can't wait to soak up the sun. I fantasize about watching ocean waves crash onto a shore for the first time in thirteen years. Bubbles and sidewalk chalk will entertain Ivy when I need to work remotely.

We purchase our tickets and eagerly await March.

A few weeks before our scheduled vacation, Ivy exhibits coughing spells. A few days before we leave, she spikes a fever. The COVID-19 virus that was slowly infiltrating the United States did not occur to me. According to the random news bits I acquired, the coronavirus was afflicting people who had traveled outside of the country, mostly on the West coast. It hadn't reached Minnesota yet, right? [72]

March 11, 2020: The coronavirus is declared a pandemic by the World Health Organization. North Dakota (our neighbor state) announces its first coronavirus case. Trump initiates a European travel ban. The US State Department advises citizens reconsider travel *abroad*. Our flight to Pensacola leaves

---

72. False. The first COVID case was identified in Minnesota on March 6th.

in the morning; our return flight is scheduled for three weeks later.

"Are you having second thoughts?" my mom asks.

Panicked Americans hoard resources and cancel international flights. But I am desperate to escape the doldrums of home life. Ivy's fever has resolved, and we'll be flying domestic. How bad could it get?

"I'm still game if you are."

§

March 12th: "Walt Disney World Resort in Florida announces it will close at the end of the business day Sunday through the end of the month." The Fargo and Minneapolis airports are quieter than usual. A few passengers wear masks. We land in Pensacola late at night and settle in at Lori's house.

March 13th: "Walz declares state of emergency for Minnesota, urges cancelling or postponing all large events." We drive to Target to stock up on food and other essentials for our vacation.

Text from Derek: Sounds like more and more shit is closing and being canceled

Me: Yeah, good thing Disneyworld wasn't on the agenda! We hit Target today, but it was pretty chill in there. Going to the beach in the morning before they close those!

Derek: What? Are they talking about closing the beaches?

Me: No, just thinking of possibilities

§

My mom and I laugh with Lori about my vacation curse. We wonder if the lifted curse had been an illusion.

Lori says, "Everything will be perfect on this trip."

March 14th: My mom, Ivy, and I visit Fort Pickens beach, clearing out in the early afternoon to avoid the spring breakers. Later that evening, we go to Barnes and Noble and I buy a book club novel: *Station Eleven*, a story about a pandemic.

March 15th: "Fauci: No 'immediate' need for domestic travel ban." Local schools back home close until the end of March. We go to the dollar store and fresh market to buy more supplies, apply plenty of hand sanitizer.

Derek: Incubation period is up to 14 days. So…when you guys get back, none of us are going anywhere for 2 weeks.

Me: I feel like things might be different by then.

Derek: Hopefully!

…

Microsoft Fargo[73] is closed until further notice.

March 16th: "Minnesota orders temporary closure of restaurants, bars and other public places." "WWE will hold Wrestlemania 36 in an empty Orlando arena." Ivy collects seashells at Navarre Beach. We stop at a souvenir shop on our drive back to Lori's house.

Derek: How is today going? Work is falling apart. Everyone is connecting through VPN and it's too much for the system.

Me: Today has been pretty good except for the reminder that little swimmers do not contain pee.

Diapers I mean.

---

73. Derek's place of work

Ivy had pee running down her leg at a souvenir shop.

§

I recently flew alone for the first time in my life. Leading up to my trip, I told Derek

"I'm scared. I've never flown without my mommy before."

I was being silly but also telling the truth. I can only assume my ability to keep my panic in check during the budding pandemic was because I didn't have to be *the* adult. I out-sourced my worries to my mom who started panicking soon-er than I did.

In addition, I survived the Swine flu, a virus considered more dangerous for my age group. Coronavirus wasn't problem-atic for children or healthy, young adults. Only unhealthy smokers and the elderly could die from it, right? [74]

I blame Trump for my ignorance. Not because he claimed the coronavirus was no more dangerous than the flu, but be-cause I stopped listening to MPR daily when I couldn't stand to hear to his voice anymore.

§

March 17th: "Florida cancels all remaining testing for state's schools." We spend the day chilling at my aunt's house. As I laze on a patio swing, an airplane soars above my head. *Will the sky soon be silent?*

Derek: Some businesses are not coming back from this.

March 18th: "Coronavirus in Minnesota: Backlog of 1,700 Tests Leads Gov. Walz To Ask Pence For Help." We go "down by the bay," take a beautiful hike through the woods and dig our toes in the sand. Ivy explores a deserted play-

---

74. *Wrong.* We learned so many things about the COVID virus, so fast.

ground.

Derek: I miss you guys but I'm glad you are where you are at. Best possible scenario for all of you.

How are things today?

Me: Good aside from the world falling apart around us.

Derek: Yeah, strange times.

March 19th: "Why a top Harvard doctor is calling for a 'national quarantine' to stem the effects of the coronavirus pandemic." We wear disposable masks, embark on another supply run. Limits are imposed on crucial items like bottled water and toilet paper. My mom searches for rubbing alcohol so we can sanitize everything we purchase, but it's sold out.

Derek: …If it looks like there will be a lockdown, you guys need to be ready to rent a car and drive back in less than 24 hours.

In California they are already beginning to restrict movement

Me: Do you want us to come home if they cancel flights?

Derek: I want you to make that decision now. If they cancel them for 2 weeks what happens if it's extended to 4. When do you come back?

What's the plan? We need one. Figure it out and let me know.

In Lori's backyard, Ivy splashes around a white inflatable pool with bright yellow lemons on the side. She sips ice cold lemonade out of a purple plastic cup. When life hands you lemons—

"Florida governor to spring breakers: get off the beaches."

March 20th: Some local beaches close due to spring breakers ignoring social distancing guidelines. We go to Navarre beach, discuss the escalating situation. Ivy flies a sun kite with her stuffed bear, Corduroy, by her side. She sports a blue tongue after indulging in her first shaved ice. I bought her the blue raspberry flavor, my childhood favorite, because decisions are even harder when you're stressed.

My mom and I fret over our current dilemma. We don't want to go home, where it's 50 degrees colder and real life awaits us. Watching the waves quells our worries, the sun melts our fears—

"Navarre Beach to close starting at midnight." How can I pretend the pandemic isn't real without the promise of a regular beach escape? I finally start to panic. Derek is way ahead of me.

"If something happens to me, I want you and Ivy to be here," he pleads over the phone.

§

I'd be remiss if I didn't interrupt this piece for an important message. I had the luxury of being on vacation while the pandemic upended American life as we knew it. Rather than fearing the COVID virus itself, I was more concerned with how my mental health would fare being trapped inside back at home. Concerts I had been looking forward to were cancelled. Programs providing free entertainment for my toddler would no longer be an option. Virtual friend dates would replace sharing a microphone during bar karaoke. My life would soon resemble the endless repeats reminiscent of *Groundhog's Day*.

However, after my trip, the pandemic will not affect my finances and my family will have the means to order groceries via Instacart. We won't have to leave the house for work or learn how to navigate online classes. We will have the comfort of health insurance if hospitalization becomes necessary. I will be at the top of the vaccine list because I'm a clinical dietitian at a long-term care facility. How was I able to remain calm for so long? Denial and ignorance were certainly part of it, but then of course there's this: I'm a lucky, privileged sonofabitch.

§

March 21st: Rumors circulated: Minnesota will issue a shelter-in-place order soon. My mom and I can't stomach the possibility of getting trapped in Pensacola, of being hospitalized in a red state. We agree to cut the trip short but wish to avoid germ-infested airports. We'll cancel our flights after we get home. Rental car acquired. My mom is the only one allowed to drive, according to the rental company policy. She is terrified and exhausted at the notion of steering this ship alone.

March 22nd: We're going on a Mad Max road trip and we're bringing anxiety. We're going on a Mad Max road trip and we're bringing anxiety and beer. We're going on a Mad Max road trip and we're bringing anxiety, beer, and Clorox wipes. We leave in the early morning. From Pensacola to Birmingham, Alabama. Gray, cloudy skies and my mom's clammy hands on the steering wheel. Northbound through Tupelo, Mississippi, to Memphis. Falling temps and distant mountains.

Ivy dances her Peppa Pig figures on the edge of her car seat. Potty training can wait. I don't want her touching *anything* inside a rest area. I change Ivy's diapers in the car and slather her hands with sanitizer. Twelve full hours cramped inside a vehicle, we hit our limit and settle in at a Drury (appropriate) hotel in Cape Girardeau, Missouri.

My mom and I rejoice over free lukewarm baked potatoes provided by the hotel. We spend the better part of an hour trying to open my mom's (much-needed) beer bottle without an opener. Maybe this robe hook? How about this plastic

Kleenex box holder? An ironing board? I nearly sprain my wrist trying to twist the cap off barehanded, determined to complete this quest. My mom finally MacGyvers the bottle open using a closet door hinge. Hallelujah! One small step for man, one giant leap for my mom's sanity.

March 23rd: We leave the hotel before dawn. My mom white knuckles the steering wheel past St. Louis. Northwest through Iowa. Adrenaline, endless snacks, and limitless tablet time for the child sustain us. Then on to Sioux Falls, South Dakota. The end is in sight! But the contrast between the warm, sunny days left behind and the dirt speckled piles of snow greeting us dampens our spirit. We finally reach Moorhead, Minnesota, around 10pm that evening. Home sweet home?

March 25th: Derek and I watch *Outbreak*, a 1995 pandemic film starring Dustin Hoffman.

March 26th: I drive my mom to her house in Fergus Falls, Minnesota, thankful to get out of my house for a few hours. We linger during our goodbye hug, not sure when we'll see each other again.

March 27th: "Florida Orders Roadblocks to Stop Virus Spreading from Louisiana."

"Emergency Executive Order 20-20 Directing Minnesotans to Stay at Home: Beginning on Friday, March 27, 2020 at 11:59 pm through Friday, April 10, 2020 at 5:00 pm, all persons currently living within the State of Minnesota are ordered to stay at home or in their place of residence..."

I didn't go on any more trips that year.

W

is for Weight

I was a late bloomer to the famous freshman 15. It didn't come for me until my fourth year of college, in 2009. My weight gain didn't bother me at first. I had started eating healthier according to my new and improved eating standards. Author and real food activist Michael Pollan[75] taught me processed food was the root of all evil, so I tried to incorporate as many whole foods into my diet as possible. I may have taken his permission to eat butter a little too seriously.

My weekdays often started with a farmer's breakfast: 2 eggs fried in butter and oatmeal made with organic whole milk, sweetened with real maple syrup. I purchased a custom trail mix sold at Tochi's, a local health food store, and blended it with enough peanut oil to achieve a smooth consistency. This invention made me proud, and I ate it almost every day, slathered on dense homemade barley bread. These recurrent heavy meals would have been harmless if I tended fields for a living. Instead, I rode the bus to my college campus and sat on my butt most of the day.

75. Yes, another Michael Pollan reference. Listen, I can't help that he's brilliant.

Recently released from the shackles of a codependent relationship, hints of sunlight started streaming through my dreaded existence. I lived in an apartment above Megan, one of my best friends. On the weekends, we often took shots of Svedka vodka and biked in a delirious state to our favorite dive bar, The Empire. My new boyfriend Derek and I made elaborate brunches: buckwheat pancakes covered with peanut butter and syrup, with crispy bacon slices on the side. We washed down our meal with a rich fruit smoothie (also containing peanut butter). Then we lazed about on his bed, exploring the peaks and valleys of each other's bodies. This hedonist lifestyle seemed overdue. I didn't think about calories.

But then, an assignment ruined everything. While attending North Dakota State University for dietetics, my classmates and I assessed each other's body fat compositions. The assignment served as a trial run of skills we might use with future clients.

My class partner used body fat calipers to measure various parts of my body: bicep, thigh, abs. Then I plugged those numbers into a formula and discovered my body fat was above the ideal amount for health. I glanced around at the other students. Most, if not all of them, were skinnier than me. I never noticed before. It seemed irrelevant, inconspicuous even until asked to strip down and have our bodies scrutinized by plastic devices. For the first time in my life, calories mattered.

I didn't want to change my diet. Too complicated. Though healthy eating was my goal, I often overate for fun and as a coping mechanism for stress. Setting a limit on calories didn't seem like a realistic option. Counting calories is also easier when you eat predominantly prepackaged foods. You can check a soup can for nutrition info and plug it into an online calorie counter. But if you are making soup from scratch, you must enter each individual ingredient. Ain't nobody got time for that! Instead, I focused on burning calories through exercise. When it comes to exercise, more equals better, right?

Shortly after the school year ended, I moved into a new apartment. That summer, I biked approximately two miles from my downtown Fargo apartment to my sandwich factory job (Subway).

I stored my bike in my apartment. At my previous residence, someone stole my precious silver Haro, a BMX bike I had no business owning. Its replacement was a cheap piece of junk that I used as a primary mode of transportation.

I carried my mountain bike down a flight of stairs and sailed onto the sidewalk at 5:30am. Then I worked on my feet for 8 hours, lugging trays of bread and boxes of produce around when I wasn't busy helping customers. At 2pm, I biked home against gusting prairie winds, then carried my wheels back up the stairs.

My stomach growled as I walked inside. I ate a small veggie sandwich for lunch and had a banana during my break, but that was hours ago. I rubbed my eyes and changed out of my uniform into shorts and a t-shirt. *I shouldn't have stayed up so late.* After popping the Tae-bo VHS into my VCR, I tied my running shoes. My stomach growled again while my cheerleader, Billy Blanks, greeted me through the TV. For the next hour, buckets of sweat streamed down the back of my neck.

When I finished my workout, I headed to the kitchen and stuffed my face full of anything in sight. I collapsed on the floor and zoned out in front of the television, perhaps watching reruns of *Survivor Man*. The next day, I would do it all over again. I lost seven pounds and hit a plateau. Then winter came, and I turned to ice cream as an antidepressant for my seasonal affective disorder. I gained all the weight back—and then some.

Fast forward to 2011. Derek and I started going to the gym together. I experimented with cooking more plant-based meals. We lost a little weight. Eventually, persistent gut issues pushed me to adopt a strict elimination diet in a desperate attempt to feel better. My weight loss surged after embarking on this pseudo-starvation diet. I can't remember my exact menu, but there were a lot of rice cakes involved. I likely ate half the calories I needed.

People at work offered compliments, and I didn't know how to respond. I wanted to lose weight—but not like this. I'm reminded of a Tig Notaro joke from her famous Largo set where she announced her (very) recent cancer diagnosis.[76] While recovering from C-diff (a horrible intestinal infection) and grieving the recent death of her mother, she stood with her shirt off awaiting a mammogram. The technician said, "Oh my gosh, you have such a flat stomach. What is your secret?" To which Tig replied, "Oh— I'm dying."

My stomach shrunk along with my body, making it difficult to eat large meals. Even after letting go of my super-strict diet, smaller, plant-based meals remained a constant. I decided to try more diets to deal with my unresolved stomach pain. Though weight loss was not the goal, additional weight melted off as I dedicated myself to these different eating patterns. I dropped down to the lowest weight I had ever been and was not impressed. My limbs appeared atrophied, and my curves disappeared. According to the criteria I learned in college, I was one pound below my "ideal" body weight.

I lost my period for several months, and yet, this didn't concern me. I was at a "healthy" weight for my height per BMI, so I figured everything was fine. BMI stands for body mass

_____

76. You've never heard it? Go listen to it right now!

index. It *can* be a helpful tool for assessing appropriate weight status, but I used my healthy BMI as an excuse to be an absolutist. My amenorrhea suggested my body had its own definition of a healthy weight I failed to meet.

§

You don't need to be neurotic to fret over your weight. If you live in a developed western country and identify as female, weight obsession is considered normal. American women are never allowed to be satisfied with their bodies. No matter how many bowls of porridge we eat, we struggle to find our Goldilocks weight, the one that's "just right." Thin women desire curves, medium-built women strive for their high school or pre-mom figures, and plus-sized women want all those skinny bitches to shut the fuck up. Of course, not *every* western woman is preoccupied with her weight and plenty of men are self-conscious about their bodies too, but this modern pressure on women to achieve an "ideal" weight is insidious and undeniable.

In her book, *The Ministry of Thin*, Emma Woolf states: "Self-deprecating comments about our appearance are a shortcut to female friendship." My female friends are sexy, smart, feminist ladies, but guess what? They all worry (or have worried) about their weight. *All of them.* Friend A struggled with bulimia. Friend B and I commiserated over our arm fat. We laughed about how she positioned her arms away from her body to appear thinner in photographs. Friend C follows a ketogenic[77] diet to manage her weight. Friend D and I cursed our stubborn belly fat. How much easier it would be to wear maternity jeans for the rest of our lives than deal with our muffin tops. Friend E berates herself for the pounds she's gained since having kids. Friend F and I worked out at the gym together. Perpetually creating fitness plans to follow—no really, we mean it this time—starting

---

77   Very low-carb diet

tomorrow. The list goes on.

Knowledge is power, but when it comes to achieving a desired weight, it can't compete. Though we may be smart enough to identify this desire as based on propaganda, our wishes remain the same. We know it's ridiculous to obsess over something so trivial. But efforts to control our weight allow us to feel powerful in a world where we often feel powerless.

The perfect weight is an intoxicating fantasy to work toward, a distraction from the everyday blahs. It's a symbol of who we once were or everything we know we could be! And who's to say if we all lost those last five pounds, our collective joy wouldn't be the catalyst for achieving world peace?

§

I started eating more calories after piecing together which foods wouldn't trigger my stomach pain. I gained a few pounds before getting married in September of 2012, and my period returned. I remember gazing at my body in the mirror, excited to see some curves reemerge.

My weight shot back up in no time. Now I had too many curves, in places I didn't approve of. Mostly I dealt with it by complaining, but I also made a few efforts to fix it, including a short stint with calorie counting.

In 2016, I found peace with my weight during pregnancy. Gaining weight didn't bother me. The baby within me needed calories to grow. Sick of focusing on my own health, I was eager to take care of someone else for a change, and I wore my belly with pride. And thanks to breastfeeding and lugging a little person around all day, I quickly lost the baby weight and then some.

My responsibility as a mother includes liking my body, or at least pretending like I do. I don't want my daughter to witness me pinching my love handles with disgust or swearing when I step on a scale. American advertising will force her to evaluate her body in relation to others. She doesn't need a mom who encourages her to do the same.

My weight has been up, down, and all around over the past several years. These days I don't focus on the shape of my body (much). I like to tell myself those silly preoccupations with my weight are behind me, but I know better than that. I am an American woman, after all.

X

is for X-Rated

Let's talk about sex ba-by, let's talk about ther-a-py. Pretty sure that's how the song goes.

§

"Waaaaaahh," my 18-month-old daughter wails from my bedroom. I bolt out of the bathroom to rescue her.

"What's wrong, sweetie?"

She approaches me with tears in her eyes, cradling a trembling pink toy she must have turned on by accident.

Oh—I see you've found my vibrator.

§

The first time I sexually experimented, I was 5 years old. My friend Natalie and I debated over who would play "the boyfriend" and decided to take turns. I pulled down my underwear to let her kiss my mons pubis and labia majora (it was all a "vagina" back then). She laughed in between kisses, highlighting the fact we were confused children with the vague notion genitals were "private" and therefore, forbidden and exciting. But also, *haha—vagina!*

Two years later, I set up an elaborate plan to kiss my friend Beth, creating a scene where we ran around a "building" (a large appliance box) and our lips just happened to run into each other. Somewhere in this plan, I convinced her to remove her shirt as well.

Shortly after this, I felt the need to come clean. Sexual feelings were *embarrassing* and certainly not appropriate for kids. During a bath, I confessed pieces of these events to my mom as shame spread through my body. The response I received was loud and clear: don't do that again.

Inside a sleeping bag, I pseudo-masturbated around the age of 7. There may have been some play commentary that my older sister overheard on the other side of the room.

"What are you doing?" Louisa demanded, a tone of disgust in her inquiry.

The message I received was loud and clear: don't do that again.

Catholicism taught me the sterilized notion of sex looking like a married couple having sex in the dark to create more of God's children.

Casual sex was:

DIRTY

DANGEROUS

AN ABOMINATION

Lesson learned: sexual desire is *wrong*.

While watching *Ghost*, my parents instructed me to hide behind the recliner during the pottery scene. When Forrest and Jenny make love[78] in *Forrest Gump*, my Catholic maternal grandmother squirmed, prompting my sister and me to fast-forward. These movies were rated PG-13.

Most of the sexual media I absorbed as a child were the unedited bits of whatever was showing on cable television. As a result, I witnessed overemphasized elements of coercion and male pleasure. At the beginning of *Romancing the Stone*, a woman is held at gunpoint while a dirty cowboy demands she take off her clothes. In *Abducted*,[79] a deranged mountain man kidnaps and sexually assaults a female jogger. These movies were rated PG.

When I was twelve, I locked my bedroom door and muted my 19-inch television to watch late-night soft-core porn on Cinemax. I tried to trick myself into thinking I wanted to teach myself what was expected of me, sexually. I wasn't depraved, this was research! Apparently, pubic hair was undesirable because these ladies didn't have any.

X-rated movies hid behind a curtain at the video rental store. Years after tricking Beth into kissing me, I suggested we rent the horror classic *I Spit on Your Grave*[80] because the description promised a rape and revenge tale. Not fucked up at all, huh? I was so desperate to view sex in a socially acceptable manner I had to rely on Hollywood's exploitation of women, cloaked in an innocent desire to watch a scary movie. America loves their murder porn.

---

78. Full disclosure: I detest this phrase, but how else can you describe this tender scene?

79. Courtesy of *USA Up All Night*

80. Spoiler alert: If you've never seen this movie, I suggest you keep it that way. The rape scenes are extensive and brutal and watching it made me ill. Eventually, you get to witness the victim cut off one of the offending dicks though. So yeah, it's a Rape and Revenge story with capital R's.

I remember talking to my mom about sex exactly twice as a teenager. As I rummaged around the refrigerator for a snack, she caught me off guard.

"I saw on Oprah that kids in junior high are giving oral sex in school bathrooms. Do you know anything about this?"

"Uhh—"

I hadn't even kissed a boy yet.

The next conversation happened in the car around the age of 15. My mom told me whenever I decided to start having sex, to be sure and get on the pill first:

"No daughter of mine is getting pregnant in high school."

Good talk, mom.

My academic sexual education was not much better. In my sixth-grade health class, I received an assignment to write a letter to my future spouse, promising to "save myself" for him.[81] During my tenth-grade health class, boys were instructed to stand on one side of the room while girls stood on the other side.[82] We scribbled down STDs on sheets of paper and then walked toward each other in pairs.

"I just gave you syphilis," I sheepishly announce to my classmate.

"And I am giving you herpes," they reply.

From the novelty store Spencers, my male friend stole a white vibrator for me that looked like a medical device. I didn't ask him to, but he had a crush on me, and maybe this was his way of wooing me? Perhaps I could self-educate. I attempted to masturbate, turning the vibrator on, and pushing it in and out of my vagina, mechanically. *What is supposed*

---

81. I was living in the South at the time.

82. The design of this lesson was inherently problematic: Where would a non-binary student stand?

to be so great about this? I didn't understand the difference between a vulva and a vagina or where the clitoris was or how it worked or what to do— so I gave up on masturbation and eventually tossed the vibrator in an apartment dumpster.

§

All American women grow up facing the virgin/whore dichotomy: you should be pleasing to look at and accommodate men's desires, but if you explore your own sexual inclinations, you're a hussy. You can read all about it in *The Purity Myth* by badass Jessica Valenti if you want to be woke.

Thanks to Catholic indoctrination and America's deranged views toward sex, I approach watching porn with a *look-over-your-shoulder, because your parents might catch you* vibe, even as a married thirtysomething year old.

Most porn is created with men in mind, and the industry is problematic. But women like porn too, and there's even some created by and for women. The *Fifty Shades of Grey* series is popular for a reason (despite the horrendous writing). I'm a feminist who doesn't want to support raunchy old men, but I'm also a human being with the ability to watch people have sex in the comfort of my own home. What's a girl to do?

§

From a naughty NSFW subreddit, I click on various videos, equally enthralled and horrified.

People get off on this? I wonder aloud, clicking on "Stepdad Fucks Stepdaughter on Kitchen Table."

Suddenly, my sinful quest is interrupted by an official-looking message: my computer has been compromised, and I need to call the number on the screen to fix it. Obviously, a Microsoft message, created by Windows staff! Well shit, this didn't look good.

I should call my husband Derek to verify this sketchy pop-up. He works at Microsoft and knows computers in a way I never will. He also knows I occasionally look at porn, so it wouldn't be a total shock. But I'm embarrassed by the content I clicked on and prefer to erase the laptop memory when I'm done, so I'll just solve this issue on my own.

I dial the number and await my fate. When a man answers the phone, there is excessive background noise which strikes me as odd, but he sounds official enough. He has a strong Indian accent, and I try to push any stereotypical assessments out of my mind. Microsoft has offices all around the globe, after all.

I tell him my plight, reading off the message on my computer screen.
"It looks like you were looking at some adult content."
I want to die right now. "Yeah…"
"It's only natural. I can direct you to some websites that are safer to visit in the future."
"No, this has ruined porn for me. I'm never looking at it ever again!"
He butters me up, making my shame less palpable. Then, he gets down to business.

The man directs me to a help site where he pretends (I later learn) to log into a staff Microsoft account (he's good) and proceeds to take control of my computer.

Occasional red flags pop up during our conversation, making me question the validity of this whole operation, but then he says or does something convincing, restoring my confidence.[83]

Apparently, I need to buy a firewall program to solve the problem. The cost is somewhere around $100 or $200. *Two hundred dollars and this all goes away?* Worth it.

Then I do the unthinkable. I give this man my credit card info. To my credit (heh), I use a card with a low credit limit that isn't tied to my bank account. So, I'm a dummy, but a cautious one at least.

The man keeps prompting me to purchase additional bells and whistles.
"I can't afford that. I just want the issue resolved as soon as possible."
After several minutes, he gives up and tells me to await a phone call from their billing department for confirmation.

I call Derek to confess and explain the situation to see if I had been duped. You bet I had.

"They have control of my computer, and they're processing payment now—"
"Shut off your computer."
"Shut it down?"
"Shut it off right now."
"Ahhh, okay!"
I plead my case, "They were so convincing!"
"Yeah, I've seen some of those. They've gotten really good."

Derek tells me to call my credit card company to try and get

---

83. I obtained my first smartphone in 2016. This is the level of technology literacy we're dealing with here.

the charges reversed. During a three-way call with Capital One and the scammer "company," I accuse them of such. They assure me they are a legit operation and would be happy to reimburse me.

After some investigation, Derek determined they were trying to sell themselves as a credible organization, so he wasn't too concerned they would try to steal information off my computer, but of course, we updated our security, changed passwords, etc. to be safe.

Wisdom garnered: You'll pay for giving in to your sexual curiosities, ya heathen!

§

Is it any wonder I didn't have my first orgasm until I was in my twenties? When my friend Kaitlin discovered this, she was horrified.

"We're going to buy you a vibrator and I'm going to wait outside your bedroom door until you finish!"

That's not how it went down but I appreciated her concern. In *college*, I finally received a proper sexual education via a health course that explained how important the clitoris was and a trip to Sex World where I purchased a pink vibrator.

"Have you had an orgasm yet?" my friend Annika asked.
"I think so?"
"You'd know."
A few days later, the difference between *almost* and achieving climax became crystal clear.

Unfortunately, the ability to have an orgasm with a partner was an entirely different story. A long one, so here's a quick summary: After years of struggling to have an orgasm in Derek's presence, he encouraged me to seek out the help of a sex therapist. She recommended an informative book called *Come As You Are: The Surprising New Science That Will Transform Your Sex Life* by Emily Nagoski. The contents of this book + more sex therapy + the decision to open our marriage + dirty thirties hormones = things have improved. But there was a lot of unlearning to do, no thanks to the sex-negative culture I was raised in.

§

I laugh as I reclaim my vibrator from my scared toddler. *Whoops! I guess I forgot to put that away.*

I aim to raise my daughter in a sex-positive household. Not too long ago, I heard her singing a song from the bathtub that made me proud:

"This is the way I wash my vulva, wash my vulva, wash my vulva. This is the way I wash my vulva so early in the morning."

A vulva and a vagina are not the same thing? Who knew?

Y

is for Yo-Yo Dieting

During the 3rd grade, I was intrigued by a health unit called Hearty Heart. We watched animated movie clips that introduced new heroes, including Dynamite Diet and Flash Fitness. Coloring sheets were issued, featuring the villain Food Fat. This unit appealed to my inherent fixation on correctness, and I applied this knowledge when I started packing my own lunches in middle school. They were always "balanced" by my definition: a sandwich, a salty snack, a fruit, a vegetable, and something sweet.

In high school, my regular lunches consisted of a blueberry bagel with cream cheese or a submarine sandwich. In the cafeteria sub line, the limp turkey slices disturbingly resembled wet socks. As a result, I stuck to plain veggie subs consisting of white American cheese and shredded lettuce. Healthy eating wasn't a huge focus at the time, but if you had asked me then, I did an alright job. I didn't understand why some kids wanted to eat Domino's pizza every day and then follow that grease bomb with a chocolate sprinkle-coated doughnut for dessert. *Gross.*

During my early college days, I subsisted on trail mix, oatmeal, bananas, and Subway sandwiches. It seemed Hearty Heart's menacing enemy, Food Fat, still prowled the grocery aisles, so I decided to help others wrangle him in. I changed my major from undeclared to dietetics: a career which specializes in a reductionist approach to nutrition.

In high school, my doctor diagnosed me with IBS (irritable bowel syndrome, also known by its other sexy name: "spastic colon,") but my symptoms didn't start to affect my quality of life until my third year of college. Research suggests people with IBS have hypersensitive nerves in their digestive system. This causes normal gut processes to produce abnormal symptoms, including abdominal pain.

Eating a bowl of oatmeal left me defeated, doubled over with a stabbing sensation in my intestines. According to the IBS literature I read, oatmeal was supposed to be a "safe" choice. Yet, violent spasms forced me into submission. I wrapped my arms around my gut while grimacing in bed, staring at the ceiling. *Why me?*[84]

During this same year, breaking up with a long-term boyfriend left me starved of endorphins, and dietary research encouraged me to see food in black-and-white terms. Some foods, like oatmeal, were "good." Other foods, like ice cream, were "bad," and I wished to eradicate these from my diet. It was a perfect storm. I used food as an emotional crutch while condemning myself from eating all the foods I craved. I strived to eat healthy food that wouldn't inspire IBS flares.

§

Fuck it. At 8pm, I bundled up and drove several miles across town to purchase a pint of ice cream in the middle of winter.

---

84. If you can relate to this scene, do yourself a favor and buy some peppermint extract supplements. Those things changed my life!

I savored the first few bites, chewy cookie dough chunks mingling with the sweet frozen cream. When the Ben & Jerry's container was 2/3 empty, my belly was stuffed. *This isn't enough to save* I rationalized, shoving the spoon back into my mouth. Nausea and shame spread through my body as I stared at the melted remnants at the bottom of the cup. *Ugh. I did it again. As of tomorrow, I am cutting out ALL sugar.*

The next day I would find a loophole in my plan. *Tomorrow is a holiday—my birthday—my friend's birthday—Monday? I'll cut out all sugar after that. It's best to start a new diet on a Sunday or even the 1ˢᵗ of the month. In the meantime, I better eat as much as I can before my puritan lifestyle kicks in.* Back to the grocery store.

§

While watching *Food Matters*, a documentary about the importance of whole food nutrition, I shoved Newman O's (organic mint flavored cookies) into my mouth, one after the other. I found a certain satisfaction in watching health documentaries while indulging in junk food, as if I could repent while sinning, erasing some of the guilt. I knew what healthy eating was supposed to look like. I figured I'd get around to it eventually.

To no one's surprise, binging on sweets did not help my stomach feel better. I became obsessed with figuring out which food intolerances plagued me. My notebooks became cluttered with detailed food diaries and various lists of foods to avoid. I wrote down as many clues as possible, hoping a pattern would emerge.

I experimented with a "cleanse" that resulted in heart palpitations, a menu of raw foods that hurt my insides, and a self-imposed elimination diet that led to excessive weight loss. The recommendation for the average dieter is to lose no more than one pound per week. I lost double that amount over several weeks. I had reached the point where I chose hunger over pain, eating as little as possible to avoid upsetting my hypersensitive gut.

My stomach troubles endured. I decided to try more diets on for size, combining my personal goal of finding relief with an exercise in dietary empathy: gaining an appreciation for those who must follow restricted diets in the name of health. In 2012, I named myself "The Hungry Guinea Pig" and started a blog to chronicle my journey.

Some of the diets I followed:

1. A low-histamine diet

2. A low-sugar and yeast diet

3. A strict religious diet based on Jainism

4. A low-fructose diet

5. The Feingold diet: a diet which eliminates food dyes and salicylates, designed to treat ADHD

6. A low copper diet used to treat a rare illness called Wilson's disease

7. A Paleo diet

8. A locavore diet

9. Dysphagia diets: altered texture diets offered to people who cannot chew/swallow properly.

10. A low-tyramine diet

11. Hypoallergenic diets, eliminating the top eight most common allergens

12. A strict gluten-free diet

My menu constantly evolved to meet the demands of whatever diet took center stage in my experiment. Initially, I imposed an extra restriction on myself: I could not eat animal products sourced from a factory farm. This meant eating primarily vegan, especially at social events and restaurants, where the options often failed to meet my special criteria.

My disordered eating had simply changed form. Instead of learning to listen to my body, I followed the diets strictly in the name of project integrity. I continued to binge on whatever foods were allowed on any given diet. No sweets allowed? No problem. I'll just eat this entire bag of tortilla chips instead.

§

Overall, the Guinea Pig endeavor turned out to be a good learning experience. I discovered the limitation of FOD-MAPS[85] was key to managing my IBS symptoms. My cousin Becca, a professional therapist, was a loyal reader of my blog. After posting about my overeating struggles, she sent me a workbook that helped me start eating more mindfully. The puzzle pieces came together, allowing me to reestablish a healthy relationship with food after a seven-year hiatus.

I consider my current relationship with food to be the healthiest it's ever been—minus the part where my guts still bum me out with all their demands. I eat a plant-based diet for environmental reasons, but I don't obsess over the foods I've decided to cut out. Healthy foods make up my main menu. I strive to eat several vegetables daily, but rarely does a day go by where I don't indulge in "junk" food as well. I rediscovered the dietary wisdom of my youth: balance is key. What's that saying again? Keep your friends close and your enemies closer? Get over here, Food Fat villain! Let's split a dessert.

---

85. An acronym used to describe specific carbohydrates which are poorly absorbed in the small intestine. Before this dietary treatment was discovered, the only things doctors could offer IBS sufferers was to "eat more fiber" and "manage stress." This advice left many, including myself, hopeless and in pain.

is for Zen (Goals)

Around the age of 9, my dad fixed me a tall chocolate malt (with extra malt) and let me peer through the clear lens of his telescope. The device stood mighty in the front yard of our yellow small-town home, directly across from a sprawling corn field. To my young mind, the field stretched on almost as wide and eternal as the sky we studied.

"There's Orion's belt!" my dad announced as my straw slurped up the melted remnants pooled on the bottom of my glass.

A meteor shower was on the horizon, and we intended to experience it firsthand. We fluffed out our red sleeping bags and settled into the grass to prepare for the night ahead.

Inside my bedroom, another big dipper covered my ceiling, spelled out in plastic glow-in-the-dark stars.

§

During adolescence, I lit Yankee candles from my collection, sat in my window and wrote journal entries and poetry. I checked out library books to study illustrations of yoga poses and listened to my mom's Yanni and John Tesh CDs.

My favorite store was Natural Wonders: a shop cloaked in calm. New Age music seeped out from each corner while a warm sandalwood scent spiraled my nostrils. I bought a new treasure each time: Celtic music[86] on cassette tape, a circular magnetic structure with several small metal dolphins sprinkled upon its surface, dolphin and manatee adoption kits, a miniature guide to the stories behind famous constellations, and other various books.

The Illustrated Dream Dictionary taught me several valuable lessons:

> 1. Avoid risk-taking behavior for six months after dreaming of a tornado. Tornadoes are a recurring dream for me, so this philosophy fit well in my life. Risk taking? Me? Ha!

> 2. Dreaming about death signals a new beginning, not something sinister. What a relief!

> 3. To stay in tune with the natural magnetic fields of the Earth, your head should face North and your feet should face South while you sleep.

I kept a dream journal for a short period but dropped the habit when it started to seem tedious. I figured my subconscious would continue sending me signals if it had something important to tell me.

Around the age of 14, I purchased the book *Clear Your Clutter with Feng-Shui* which sparked my interest in the topic.

According to Feng-Shui, the placement of items within each room of a home corresponds with specific outcomes. I took note to position the head of my bed kitty-corner to my bed-

---

86. Lorenna McKennitt's *Book of Secrets*

room door: the optimum position for ensuring safety. Thankfully, my bed didn't face toward my attached bathroom. This would zap my chi, and I simply couldn't afford that. Scrubbing and putting all the dishes away meant the "wealth corner" located in our kitchen could reach its full potential. Shortly after deep cleaning this area, my mom received an unexpected escrow check. We were believers!

I began attempting to meditate. I turned on a soothing music CD, lit some Nag Champa incense, and let my mind follow an imaginative path. My version focused less on deep breathing and more on creating art with my mind. I swam in deep seas and flew high in the sky, meeting bold colors and friendly creatures along the way. Wakeful dreams of my own design.

My attraction to the ethereal world has proven to be a beneficial antagonist against my ongoing neuroses. These peaceful preoccupations provide serene moments amongst recurrent floods of chaos. If I were less lazy and stubborn, I would meditate on a regular basis. Unfortunately, I cannot even commit to five daily minutes for the sake of anxiety maintenance. I enjoy doing yoga but have a history of failed consistency. Instead, I do something I believe to be almost as helpful in my ongoing Zen efforts.

§

After putting my wireless earbuds in, I settle into my bed to prepare for sleep. I open the YouTube app on my phone and search for *Tingle Fix ASMR,* the channel of a woman named Debbie. Hmm, which video to watch this evening? There are several contenders to choose from. During "ASMR Crinkles and Other Relaxing Sounds ~ Baking ingredients ~ Soft Spoken," Debbie gently stirs a large container of rainbow sprinkles and her slow pronunciation of "shhuu-gaar" melts my spine. Or I could watch "ASMR German Candy & Makeup Unboxing ~ Soft Spoken." When Debbie slides the tips of her periwinkle painted nails over the hot cocoa packets, my head sinks further into my pillow. But tonight, I think I'll stick with an old favorite: "ASMR Page Turning ~ Yankee Candle Magazine ~ Soft Spoken." Debbie pushes into the creases along the magazine's spine, describing holiday scents such as "Apple Spice" and "Winter Glow" in a velvety tone as my eyes grow heavy. Within minutes, I am fast asleep.

§

As a child, I held an odd secret. Certain relaxing situations lulled me into a trance. I once asked a friend of mine to slowly turn the pages of a book while I lied on the floor with my eyes closed, listening closely to the slight friction of her fingers against the paper and her light measured breathing. I watched specific scenes from movies repeatedly, including Belle investigating the west wing in *Beauty and the Beast*. I loved the delicate clink of the glass cover against the ground as she uncovered the forbidden pink rose. If a person spoke or moved in a particular way, time slowed down as my scalp prickled with a delicate numbness, and I grew fuzzy with tranquility. My enjoyment of these strange sensations embarrassed me,[87] and I assumed it was a quirk belonging to me and me alone.

Years later, while listening to an episode of *This American Life*, my ears perked up as I listened to a woman describe similar experiences. I turned up the radio in awe, shocked to learn I am far from the only person to have experienced this peculiar phenomenon: Autonomous Sensory Meridian Response (ASMR).[88] ASMR is a term used to describe a sensory experience characterized by a pleasant tingling sensation in the head and scalp, which can be triggered by sounds like

---

87. True story: I hid my ASMR habit from my husband for years.

88. The term "ASMR" was coined by a woman named Jennifer Allen in 2010.

whispering or brushing, and visual stimulus like painting or drawing.

On YouTube, there are millions of videos featuring people doing various things meant to elicit the brain tingles associated with ASMR, including: tapping fingernails on a box, the slow unwrapping of a package with an emphasis on crinkle sounds, whisper reading while turning the pages of a magazine, and role-played doctor appointments, salon visits, and library checkouts. A person without ASMR might find the videos to be helpful sleep aids or they might find them weird and/or boring. As for me, this is my current preferred method of "meditation." Instead of struggling to clear my mind and focus on my breathing, I listen to a soft-spoken lady talk about her lipstick collection. Whatever works, right?

ASMR research is in its infancy, but the limited findings have been promising. In 2018, The University of Sheffield study discovered that those who claimed to experience ASMR reduced their heart rate and showed a significant increase in positive emotions while watching the videos. Their physiological response was comparable to other relaxation methods, such as mindfulness. Another 2018 study found that ASMR videos may activate brain regions associated with experiences like social bonding and involve neurochemicals such as dopamine, oxytocin, and endorphins.

§

My other favorite tool for dealing with my neuroticism is mindfulness. While reading *The Power of Now*, I discovered a new sense of freedom by reading and believing the words: "You are not your thoughts." This phrase removed a huge burden from my shoulders, helping me reanalyze whether things must always be done a certain way.

I allowed my thoughts to tell me all kinds of lies over the years: I could make terrible things happen just by thinking them, beauty was defined by others and I needed to obey their expectations, loving someone meant sacrificing my own health and happiness, good grades and high career marks were the ultimate proof of my worthiness, and my anxiety and depression would cripple my ability to be a good parent.

The masquerading demons in my head are just neurons with an affinity for mischief. I can choose to pay attention to their shenanigans or not. Awareness of their trickery is key. I am wired to gravitate toward troubled thoughts, and achieving mindfulness is easier said than done. But at least I now have the knowledge to tell those brain cells to get a job.

Acknowledgments

Thanks to my editor, Chelsey Clammer, for breathing new life into this manuscript. For my publisher, Usher Morgan: thanks for taking a chance on an unknown weirdo.

Thank you to *Living Crue Magazine* and *Braided Way Magazine* for publishing versions of "X is for X-Rated" and "R is for Religion," respectively.

Many thanks to the Moorhead Friends Writing Group, without which this book might not exist. Special thanks to the following members who helped shape my words: Chris Stenson, Stephanie Hagen-Johnson, Lyn Stoltenow, Amber Breitbach, Tiffany Fier, Sarah Nour, Chris Lucht, Sue Quinn, and Jason Bursack.

Thank you to Jill Cadwell, Ashley Gaughan, and Tessa Torgeson for spending your time critiquing chapters of this book—and for being awesome people in general.

To Kelsey: thank you for sitting by me on the bus in kindergarten and remaining by my side all these years. For Megan: thank you for all the delicious vegetarian meals and for insisting I wear a proper winter coat, as I am incapable of taking care of myself.

To my sisters Louisa and Desirae: thank you for making my childhood fun and my adulthood easier. For Becca, my sister from another mister: thank you for helping me navigate my neuroses from a young age with wisdom and kindness.

To Derek and Ryan: thank you for weathering the storm of this unorthodox relationship with me and for loving me so well.

For my parents: your creativity inspires me, and your support sustains me. I'm grateful to be your daughter.

For Ivy: may you make peace with your genetic tendencies at a younger age than your mama. I love you more than words can say.

For everyone who has ever suffered beneath the burden of mental illness: you are not alone.

Works Cited

B is for Beauty (Rituals and Revelations)

Fugazi. "Merchandise," track 4 on Repeater, Dischord Records, 1990, compact disc.

Irby, Samantha. Wow, No Thank You. New York: Vintage Books, 2020.

C is for Cemetery

Ernst, Jackie. "Why Children Love Spooky, Dead Things." Romper. October 9, 2019, https://www.romper.com/p/why-children-love-spooky-dead-things-19199976

D is for Depression

Forrest, Emma. Your Voice in my Head. New York: Bloomsbury Publishing, 2001.

Hari, Johann. "Chemical imbalances don't cause depression—society does." New York Post. January 20, 2018. https://nypost.com/2018/01/20/chemical-imbalances-dont-cause-depression-society-does/

Hari, Johann. Lost Connections: Uncovering the Real Causes of Depression – and the Unexpected Solutions. New York: Bloomsbury Publishing, 2018.

Huijbregts, Klass, Hoogendoorn, AdriaanW, Slottje, Paulien, van Balkom Anton JLM, and Batelaan, Neeltje M. "Long-Term and Short-Term Antidepressant Use in General Practice: Data from a Large Cohort in the Netherlands." Psychother Psychosom 86, no. 6 (2017): 362–369.

Ween. "Zoloft," track #2 on Quebec. Sanctuary Records. 2003.

E is for Ethics

Pollan, Michael. In Defense of Food. New York: The Penguin Press, 2008.

Trudeau, Kevin. Natural Cures "They" Don't Want You to Know About. Elk Grove Village: Alliance Publishing Group, Inc., 2004.

F is for First Love

Aron, Nina Renata. Good Morning, Destroyer of Men's Souls. New York: Crown Publishing, 2020.

Portishead. "Sour Times" track #2 on Dummy. Go! Beat, 1994, compact disc.

G is for Genetics

Fenichel, Otto. The Psychoanalytic Theory of Neurosis. London. 1946.

Marian, Gabriela, Nica, Elena, Alina, Ionescu, Brindura, Ecaterina, and Ghinea, Diana "Hyperthyroidism--Cause of Depression and Psychosis: A Case Report. Journal of Med Life, 2, no. 4 (October–December 2009: 440–442. https://pubmed.ncbi.nlm.nih.gov/20108759/.

Petersen, Andrea. On Edge: A Journey Through Anxiety. New York: Broadway Books. 2017.

Stossel, Scott. My Age of Anxiety: Fear, Hope, Dread, and the Search for Peace of Mind. New York: Random House. 2013.

H is for Hypochondrial Tendencies

Boily, Marie-Claude, Baggaley, Rebecca F, Wang, Lei, Masse, Benoit, White, Richard G, Hayes, Richard J, and Alary, Michel. "Heterosexual Risk of HIV-

1 Infection per Sexual Act: Systematic Review and Meta-Analysis of Observational Studies." Lancet Infect Dis, 9, no. 2 (February 2009): 118–129. https://pubmed.ncbi.nlm.nih.gov/19179227/.

Wilton, James. "Putting a Number on It: The Risk from an Exposure to HIV." CATIE. Fall 2012. https://www.thebodypro.com/article/putting-a-number-on-it-the-risk-from-an-exposure-t

I is for Intrusive Thoughts

Bamford, Maria. "Maria Bamford: A Seriously Funny Comedian." Interview by Terri Gross. Fresh Air, National Public Radio, July 18, 2013. Audio. https://www.npr.org/2013/07/18/202374622/maria-bamford-a-seriously-funny-comedian

Begley, Sharon. Can't. Just. Stop: An Investigation of Compulsions. New York: Simon & Schuster. 2017.

K is for Kindergarten

Jones, Dustin. "Firearms Overtook Auto Accidents as the Leading Cause of Death in Children." NPR Health. NPR. April 22, 2022. https://health.wusf.usf.edu/npr-health/npr-health/2022-04-22/firearms-overtook-auto-accidents-as-the-leading-cause-of-death-in-children

Moe, Caitlin, and Rowhani-Rahbar, Ali. "What We Know About School Mass Shootings Since Columbine and How to Prevent Them." K-12 School Shooting Database. Center for Homeland Defense and Security: Naval Postgraduate School. September 15, 2020. https://www.seattletimes.com/opinion/what-we-know-about-school-mass-shootings-since-columbine-and-how-to-prevent-them/

"States that Allow Teachers and School Staff to Carry Guns." Crime Prevention Research Center. October 8, 2018. https://crimeresearch.org/2018/03/states-allow-teachers-staff-carry-guns/

M is for Magical Thinking

Danny Elfman. "This is Halloween," track #3 on The Nightmare Before Christmas: Original Motion Picture Soundtrack. Walt Disney Records. 1993, compact disc.

N is for Night (Bears and Scares)

Dante, Joe, director. Gremlins. Amblin Entertainment, 1984.

O is for Overachiever

Schaef, Anne Wilson. "Perfectionism is Self-Abuse of the Highest Order." Quotable Quotes. Goodreads. https://www.goodreads.com/quotes/354994-perfectionism-is-self-abuse-of-the-highest-order

"Sixth Grade (Grade 6) Social Studies Questions." Map Questions. Help Teaching. 2022. https://www.helpteaching.com/questions/Social_Studies/Grade_6

P is for Pain

Frellick, Marcia. "Brain Inflammation Seen for First Time in Fibromyalgia." Medscape. November 13, 2018. https://www.medscape.com/viewarticle/904827

Janssens, Karin A M, Zijlema, Wilma L, Joustra, Monica L, and Rosmalen, Judith G.M. "Mood and Anxiety Disorders in Chronic Fatigue Syndrome, Fibromyalgia, and Irritable Bowel Syndrome: Results From the LifeLines Cohort Study." Psychosom Med, 7, no. 4 (2015) :449–457. https://pubmed.ncbi.nlm.nih.gov/25768845/

King's College London. "Fibromyalgia Likely the Result of Autoimmune Problems." ScienceDaily. July 1, 2021. www.sciencedaily.com/releases/2021/07/210701120703.htm

Raising Hope. "The Men of New Natesville." Fox.

2011.

Ramey, Sarah. The Lady's Handbook for Her Mysterious Illness. New York: Anchor. 2021.

Community. "Repilot." NBC, 2014.

Q is for Quicksand

Kinsman, Kat. Hi, Anxiety: Life with a Bad Case of Nerves. New York: Harper Collins. 2016.

Vandergriendt, Carly. "Everything You Should Know About Refeeding Syndrome." healthline. October 10, 2017. https://ahoy-stage.healthline.com/health/refeeding-syndrome

R is for Religion

Freeman, Aaron. "Planning Ahead Can Make a Difference in the End." All Things Considered. National Public Radio, June 1, 2005. https://www.npr.org/templates/story/story.php?storyId=4675953

S is for Substance Use

Built to Spill. "Reasons," track #2 on There's Nothing Wrong with Love. Sub Pop. 1994, compact disc.

Holden, Dominic. "These Teens Are Taking a Class on Drugs That Is Definitely Not What Trump Had in Mind." BuzzFeedNews. BuzzFeed. April 16, 2018. https://www.buzzfeednews.com/article/dominicholden/these-teens-are-taking-a-class-on-drugs-that-is-definitely

Spoon. "I Summon You" track #7 on Gimme Fiction. Merge Records. 2005, compact disc.

T is for Take This Waltz

Gander, Kashmira. "Polyamory is More Common Than You Think, One in Nine Americans Have Tried It." Health: Newsweek. May 26, 2021. https://www.newsweek.com/polyamorous-relationship-one-nine-americans-study-1594618

Jenkins, Carrie. What Love Is: And What It Could Be. New York. Basic Books. 2017.

O'Reilley, Jessica. "Monogamish: The New Rules of Marriage." TEDxVancouver, January 2015, https://www.youtube.com/watch?v=0sYguTPLpHE

Perel, Esther. Mating in Captivity: Reconcilling the Erotic and the Domestic. New York: Harper. 2006.

Polley, Sarah, director. Take This Waltz. Mongrel Media and Magnolia Pictures. 2011.

V is for Vacation, Interrupted

Berlinger, Joshua, Hollingsworth, Julia, Rahim, Zamira, and Renton, Adam. "North Dakota announces its first coronavirus case", "Trump will suspend all travel from Europe to the US for next 30 days", "US raises global travel advisory, urging citizens to "reconsider" travel abroad." Coronavirus News. CNN. March 11, 2020. https://edition.cnn.com/world/live-news/coronavirus-pandemic-05-11-20-intl/h_15f81e-322ab9925b18772fc7f10cf926

Berlinger, Joshua, Hollingsworth, Julia, Rahim, Zamira and Renton, Adam. "Disney World, Disneyland Paris Resort to Close Over Coronavirus Concerns." Coronavirus News. CNN. March 12, 2020. https://www.cnn.com/world/live-news/coronavirus-outbreak-03-12-20-intl-hnk/index.html

Berlinger, Joshua, Hollingsworth, Julia, Rahim, Zamira and Renton, Adam. "Minnesota orders temporary closure of restaurants, bars and other public places," "WWE will hold Wrestlemania 36 in an empty Orlando arena." Coronavirus News. CNN. March 16, 2020. https://www.cnn.com/world/live-news/coronavirus-outbreak-03-16-20-intl-hnk/index.html

Berlinger, Joshua, Hollingsworth, Julia, Rahim, Zamira and Renton, Adam. "Florida cancels all remaining testing for state's schools." Coronavirus News. CNN. March 17, 2020. https://www.cnn.com/world/live-news/coronavirus-outbreak-03-17-20-intl-hnk/index.html

Blanks, Annie. "Navarre Beach to Close Starting at Midnight, All Santa Rosa Restaurants to go Pick-Up Only." Pensacola News Journal. March 20, 2020. https://www.pnj.com/story/news/2020/03/20/navarre-beach-close-midnight-santa-rosa-county-restaurants-go-pick-up-only/2883409001/

Callaghan, Peter. "Walz Declares State of Emergency for Minnesota, Urges Cancelling or Postponing all Large Events." MinnPost. March 13, 2020. https://www.minnpost.com/state-government/2020/03/walz-declares-state-of-emergency-for-minnesota-urges-canceling-or-postponing-all-large-events/

"Coronavirus in Minnesota: Backlog of 1,700 Tests Leads Gov. Walz To Ask Pence for Help." CBS Minnesota. March 18, 2020. https://www.cbsnews.com/minnesota/news/coronavirus-in-minnesota-backlog-of-1700-tests-leads-gov-walz-to-ask-pence-for-help/

Kay, Jennifer, Stinson, Paul, Goth, Brenna, and Appel, Adrianne. "Florida Orders Roadblocks to Stop Virus Spreading from Louisiana." Bloomberg Law: Health Law & Business. March 27, 2020. https://news.bloomberglaw.com/health-law-and-business/florida-orders-roadblocks-to-stop-virus-spreading-from-louisiana

Moore, Mark. "Fauci: No 'immediate' need for domestic travel ban." New York Post. March 15, 2020. https://nypost.com/2020/03/15/fauci-no-immediate-need-for-domestic-travel-ban/

Ramsey Pflanzer, Lydia. "Why a Top Harvard Doctor is Calling for a 'National Quarantine' to Stem the Effects of the Coronavirus Pandemic." Insider: Business. March 19, 2020. https://www.businessinsider. in/science/news/why-a-top-harvard-doctor-is-calling-for-a-national-quarantine-to-stem-the-effects-of-the-coronavirus-pandemic/articleshow/74699263.cms

Walz, Tim. "Emergency Executive Order 20-20: Directing Minnesotans to Stay at Home." State of Minnesota Executive Department. March 25, 2020. https:// mn.gov/governor/assets/3a.%20EO%2020-20%20 FINAL%20SIGNED%20Filed_tcm1055-425020.pdf

W is for Weight

Notaro, Tig. "The C-Diff Diet," track # 7 on Live. Secretly Canadian. 2013, compact disc

Woolf, Emma. The Ministry of Thin: How the Pursuit of Perfection Got out of Control. Berkeley: Soft Skull Press. 2014.

X is for X-Rated

Salt 'n' Pepa. "Let's Talk About Sex," track # 10 on Blacks' Magic. Next Plateau Records. 1991, compact disc.

Z is for Zen (Goals)

"ASMR Videos 'May Have Health Benefits,' Study Finds." BBC News. BBC. June 21, 2018. https://www. bbc.com/news/uk-england-south-yorkshire-44533297

Grant, Russell. The Illustrated Dream Dictionary. New York: Sterling Publishing. 1996.

Kingston, Karen. Clear Your Clutter with Feng-Shui. New York: Judy Piatkus (Publishers) Limited. 1999.

Richard, Craig, PhD. "First Published Study to Show Brain Activity During ASMR." ASMR University: The Art & Science of Autonomous Sensory Meridian

Response. December 23, 2018. https://asmruniversity.com/2018/12/23/asmr-research-fmri-brain-activity/

Tolle, Eckhart. The Power of Now: A Guide to Spiritual Enlightenment. Novato: New World Library. 1997.

Seigel, Andrea. "Tribes: Act Two – A Tribe Called Rest." This American Life. Public Radio International. March 29, 2013.

Made in the USA
Monee, IL
10 November 2023